Teacher Talk

The activities contained in this book have been designed to help students have fun every day as they learn important math skills. Relevant, interesting activities make math more meaningful for students and help them see the important role math plays in their lives every day. Teachers will find these activities very easy to use with their students, and with the variety of skills and concepts presented, this book is sure to please almost everyone.

Math Objectives

- To experience the relationship between mathematics and the world
- To help students see themselves as successful problem solvers
- To grow in confidence and understanding using computation skills
- To provide experiences using estimation, number sense, graphing, time, time zones, money, calendars, patterning, decimals, and fractions
- To gain confidence in and improve the skill using spatial relationships and visualization
- To gain confidence in and improve the skill of using a calculator

About the Activities

This book contains 88 individual one-page activities. The activities are arranged so that there is a different type of activity each day. Many of the activities stand alone. There are some, however, that build on each other. These activities should be done in intervals of two or three days. This is to keep students using a variety of math skills and concepts at all times rather than just touching one skill. It is best to use the activities presented in the order that they appear in the book as students will encounter the simpler activities first and then be ready for the more challenging ones later.

The variety of activities presented enables all students to experience success while learning mathematical skills. All students are afforded the opportunity to engage in some type of activity at which they can succeed. For example, some students are very good at computation, while others may find spatial relationships easier. Regardless of students' strengths or weaknesses, they will all have a chance to demonstrate their mathematical capabilities. The message should be clear that every student has math ability and can be successful.

Because they do not need many materials to support them, the activities are very easy to use. Most of them need nothing more than a copy of the activity and a pencil. Occasionally, however, a pair of scissors or a piece of string is needed. While it is never specifically requested, a calculator would be very helpful in some of the activities.

The information used in these activities is accurate. Facts and figures have been obtained from reliable sources so that the activities are truly relevant and meaningful. Students may gain insight into more than just math after they work some of the problems!

If you have a question about how to solve a problem, check the answer key (pages 89-94). The answer key contains tips for solving some of the problems as well as the answers. In some cases, the students will come up with more or different answers. After hearing students' explanation, you can decide if their thinking is or is not accurate. Teacher judgment is always a vital component of good teaching!

Name ______________________

1 to 100

The objective of this activity is to find the sum of all the counting numbers from 1 to 100. You could certainly add 1 + 2 + 3 continuing to 100 to find the sum. However, this is too much work for this problem. If you look for patterns and combinations, you can find a much shorter and easier way to solve this problem. Try to work smarter, not longer.

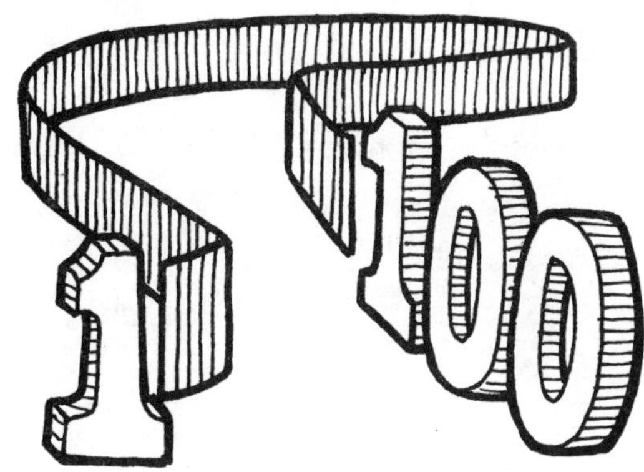

Answer 1 plus all the numbers up to 100 ______________

Now that you have found the answer to the sum of the counting numbers from 1 to 100, apply what you learned and find the sum of the counting numbers from 1 to 200.

Answer 1 plus all the numbers up to 200 ______________

Name ______________________

How Old Are You?

Everyone knows how many years old they are. Some people even quote their age to the half year. But now, you are going to find out exactly how old you are!

First count the months since your last birthday. For example, if your birthday was on October 13, then count 1 month on November 13, 2 months on December 13, etc. Then count the days since the end of the last full month you could count. Now you know your age in years, months, and days.

Years __________ Months __________ Days __________

Now, change the years to months, and you will know your age in months and days.

Months __________ Days __________

Change the months to days (use 30 days per month), and you will know your age in days. It looks like you are getting older!

Days __________

Here is a much bigger number. Change the days into hours.

Hours __________

Are you ready for the really big number? Change the hours into minutes.

Minutes ______________________

Here is the super big number! Change the minutes into seconds! Wow!!

Seconds ______________________

Did you know you were THAT old?

Name ____________________

Organize the Classes

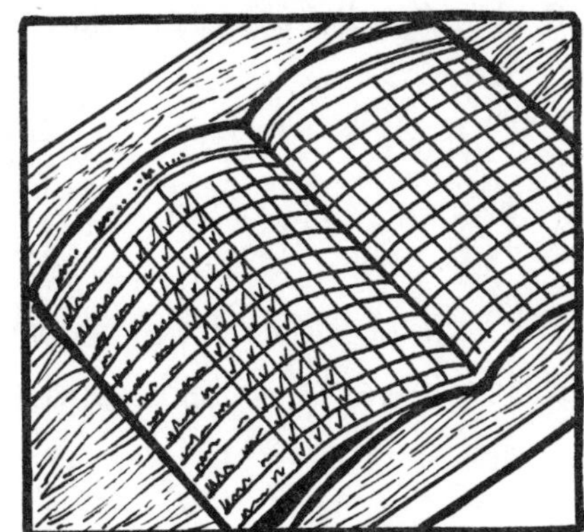

Have you ever wondered how class groupings in schools are put together? It can be a very difficult task! Students are not born in nice, neat class-size groups in each neighborhood. There might be many students of one age and few of another age. The number of teachers assigned to a school usually depends on the total number of students divided by some class number used by the school district such as 25 students per teacher.

Below are some student and teacher numbers from a small elementary school. Since all of you have been in elementary school, you have some ideas and experiences to help you try your hand at organizing the classes. Remember that classes with 30 or more students are not thought of as desirable for any grade especially in the younger grades.

There is certainly more than one way to organize these classes. Some of the factors to consider when organizing include making sure each class has students of various abilities, students of various ethnic backgrounds, and as good a balance as possible of boys and girls. Just trying to divide up these students with a balance of grades in combination classes is enough for this assignment.

First-graders: 35 students
Second-graders: 39 students
Third-graders: 29 students
Fourth-graders: 33 students
Fifth-graders: 36 students

172 students ÷ 25 students = 7 classroom teachers

Obviously there will be combination classrooms in which two grades share one teacher so you will need to think about what grades you put together. Not all classes have to be combinations. With your past experience, you will have some ideas about this, so do what you think is best for students. Since there are a variety of ways to organize these classes, be ready to explain your thinking. Maybe you will become a teacher, principal, or other school administrator and do this sort of work professionally!

Name ______________________________

Whirlybird

Start at (-12, 0). Connect each coordinate point in order going down the columns.

(-11, 5)	(-2, 4)	(14, 5)	(7, -4)	(2, -3)	(-10, -4)
(-10, 5)	(4, 4)	(5, 5)	(12, -4)	(-2, -3)	(-11, -4)
(-10, 1)	(4, 5)	(5, 4)	(12, -5)	(-2, -1)	(-11, 0)
(-9, 1)	(-5, 5)	(11, 4)	(-3, -5)	(-9, -1)	
(-9, 2)	(-5, 7)	(11, -3)	(-3, -4)	(-9, 0)	
(-2, 2)	(14, 7)	(7, -3)	(2, -4)	(-10, 0)	

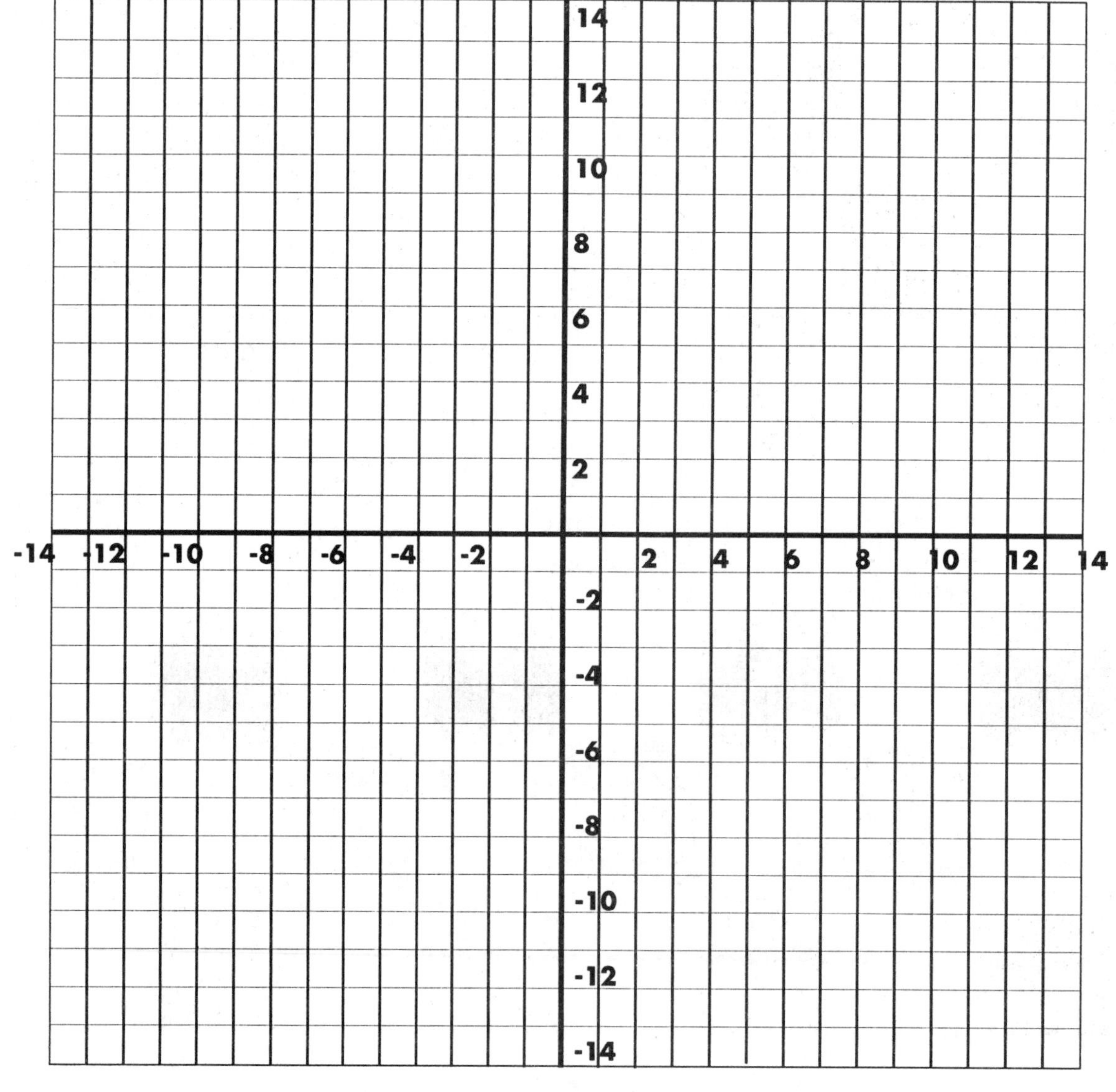

Name ____________________

Checkerboard Squares

How many squares are there on a standard checkerboard? While many of the squares are obvious, many are not. Remember to look for squares of various sizes. Also, be ready to explain your count of the squares. Happy hunting!

Number of Squares ________

Name ______________________________

Make a Triangle

Cut out the shapes on this page and put them together to make a triangle. While it is possible to make a triangle using only a few of the pieces, your challenge is to use all seven pieces to make your triangle. Yes, it is possible!

Name ______________________

A Record Flight

World records represent ultimate achievement. In the area of flying, they represent maximum performance in a specific area with competition open to all types of airplanes. It is no wonder that the holders of these records deserve and receive the greatest respect.

Two records were set on December 14-23 1986. One was for speed around the world on a nonstop, nonrefueled flight, and the other was for distance in a great circle without landing. These records were set by Americans Dick Rutan and Jeana Yeager in the plane *Voyager*. The speed record is 115.65 m.p.h., and the distance record is 24,986.727 miles.

1. These combined records represent how many hours of nonstop flying?

   ____

2. These hours represent how many days? ______________

3. The fuel tank on the *Voyager* held 4,560 liters of fuel. How many miles did the *Voyager* travel per liter? ______________

4. What was the approximate capacity of the fuel tank in gallons?

   ____

5. How many miles did the *Voyager* travel per gallon of fuel?

   ____

Name ____________________

Hey, Big Spender!

Everyone likes to spend money! Here's your chance to spend a lot of money very quickly. Pretend you have been given 1 million dollars and must spend it at the rate of $1 per second. How long will it take you to spend it all?

__________ minutes __________ seconds

or, ________ hours ________ minutes ________seconds

or, ______ days ______ hours ______ minutes ______ seconds

You have done so well that you now have been asked to spend 1 billion dollars at the rate of $1 per second. On your mark, get set, go!

__________ minutes __________ seconds

or, ________ hours ________ minutes ________seconds

or, ______ days ______ hours ______ minutes ______ seconds

or, _____ years _____ days _____ hours _____ minutes _____ seconds

Approximately how old would you be after spending 1 billion dollars this way? __________ Wow!

Name ______________________

T-Time

Cut out and assemble the shapes on this page to form a T.

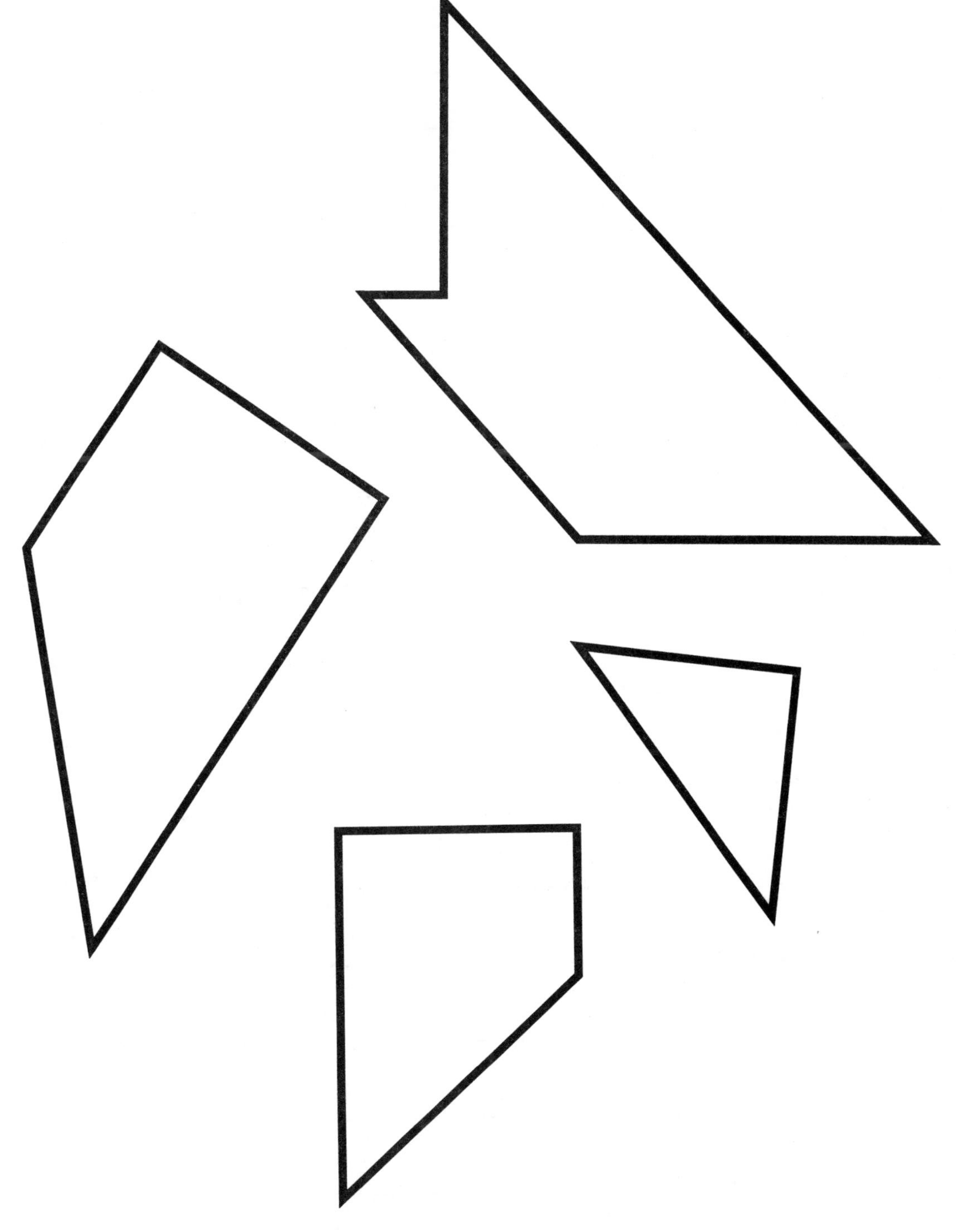

Name ____________________

Date Digits

Here's a challenge for you! How many correct number sentences can you make out of the digits of a date? Here is a sample of how to play. October 13, 1985 is usually written in short form as 10/13/85. All digits must be used once, but they can be used in any legitimate mathematical way.

101385

$8 + 1 - 1 = 3 + 0 + 5$

$8 - 3 = 5 + 1 - 1 + 0$

$5^2 = 3 \times 8 + 1 + 0 \div 1$

$\frac{10}{5} = 8 \div (3 + 1)$

Now you try it. Remember: Each number is to be used just once, and the number sentence must be correct. You may use the numbers in any way that you have learned. If you get stuck, you may use all the digits in the current year.

Your Birthday: ____________

____

____

____

____

Today's Date: ____________

____

____

____

____

Name ______________________________

Find the Area

The area for the figure below is 16 square units. To figure out the area for each of the sections, you will need to find the relationships between the sections. It will be helpful if you cut out the pieces and place them on top of each other to find the relationships involved. Memorized formulas for area will not be particularly useful in this problem.

A. The area for each section is:

1. ____ 2. ____ 3. ____ 4. ____ 5. ____ 6. ____ 7. ____

B. If the area for section 5 is 4 square units, what is the area of each section?

1. ____ 2. ____ 3. ____ 4. ____ 5. ____ 6. ____ 7. ____

The area for the whole figure is ______________________________

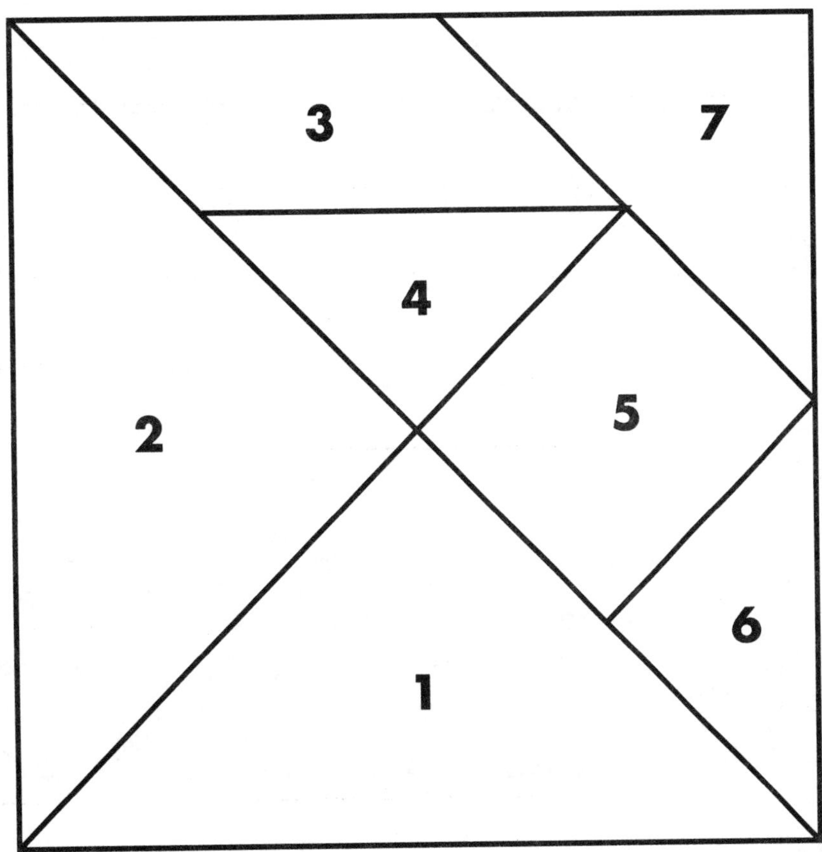

Name ______________________

Consecutive Numbers

Consecutive numbers are numbers that come in sequence without any interruption.

An example of consecutive whole numbers is 14, 15, and 16.

Challenge 1: Find three consecutive whole numbers with a sum of 144.

Answer: ______________________

An example of consecutive even numbers is 14, 16, and 18.

Challenge 2: Find three consecutive even numbers with a sum of 144.

Answer: ______________________

An example of consecutive odd numbers is 13, 15, 17, and 19.

Challenge 3: Find four consecutive odd numbers with a sum of 144.

Answer: ______________________

Name ______________________

Magic Square 1

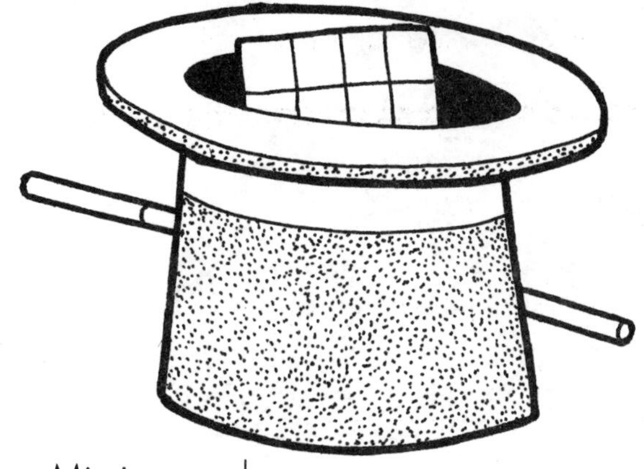

In a magic square, each row, column, and diagonal has the same sum. The magic square below has been started but not finished. Fortunately, we have the numbers that fit in the empty squares. Your task is to find the correct placement for each of these numbers. Abracadabra won't solve this magic square, but your fine mind will do a great job!

Missing numbers:

11	9	12	4
8	5	13	6

Enough numbers have been already entered in the square so that you can find out what the total of each row, line, and diagonal should be.

				Sum:
8		16		____
	12		9	____
		7	13	____
14			13	____

Sum: ____ ↙ ____ ____ ____ ____ ↘ ____

Name ____________________

Have a Heart

Everyone has a heart. The heart is a marvelous pump that circulates blood through pathways totalling over 100,000 miles to reach every part of the body. Can you imagine how long that is? Try comparing it to distances with which you may already be familiar.

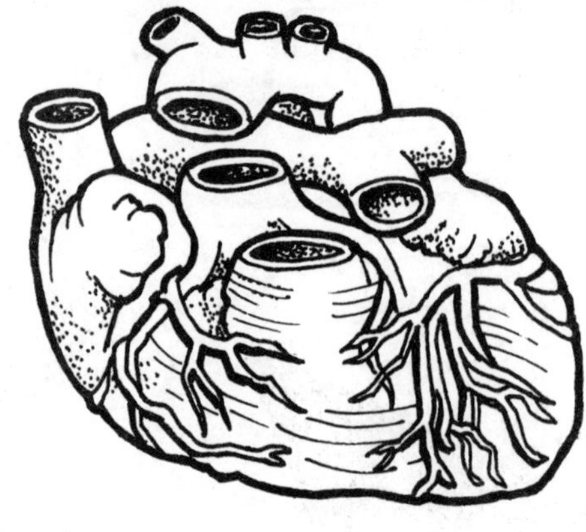

1. The distance from Los Angeles to New York City is approximately 2,900 miles. The distance your blood travels is comparable to how many trips between these two cities?

   ____

2. At the equator, the distance around Earth is approximately 25,000 miles. The distance your blood travels is comparable to how many trips around the Earth?

   ____

Your heart pumps about five quarts of blood through its chambers every 60 seconds.

3. Five quarts is equal to how many 16-ounce bottles of soda pop? ____________
4. How many gallons of blood does your heart pump in one hour? ________
5. in one day? ____________
6. in a week? ____________
7. in your lifetime? ____________________
8. A small swimming pool (20′ x 60′) will hold about 65,000 gallons of water. This represents the amount of blood pumped by your heart in approximately how many weeks? ____________________

Name ______________________________

Make a Parallelogram

Cut out the shapes on this page and put them together to make a parallelogram. While it is possible to make a parallelogram using only a few of the pieces, your challenge is to use all seven pieces to make your parallelogram. Yes, it is possible!

Name ______________________

More Consecutive Numbers

Consecutive numbers are numbers that come in sequence without any interruption.

An example of consecutive whole numbers is 22, 23, and 24.

Challenge 1: Find five consecutive whole numbers with a sum of 150.

Answer: ______________________

An example of consecutive even numbers is 22, 24, and 26.

Challenge 2: Find five consecutive even numbers with a sum of 150.

Answer: ______________________

An example of consecutive odd numbers is 23, 25, 27, and 29.

Challenge 3: Find four consecutive odd numbers with a sum of 160.

Answer: ______________________

Name ______________________

Up and Down

During one week, Houston, Texas, recorded the following high and low temperatures:

	Mon.	Tues.	Wed.	Thurs.	Fri.
High	82°	78°	81°	90°	86°
Low	72°	48°	67°	74°	69°

Using different colors to show the highs and lows, construct a bar graph displaying this information. Remember to label your graph.

Key:
High Temp. ☐
Low Temp. ☐

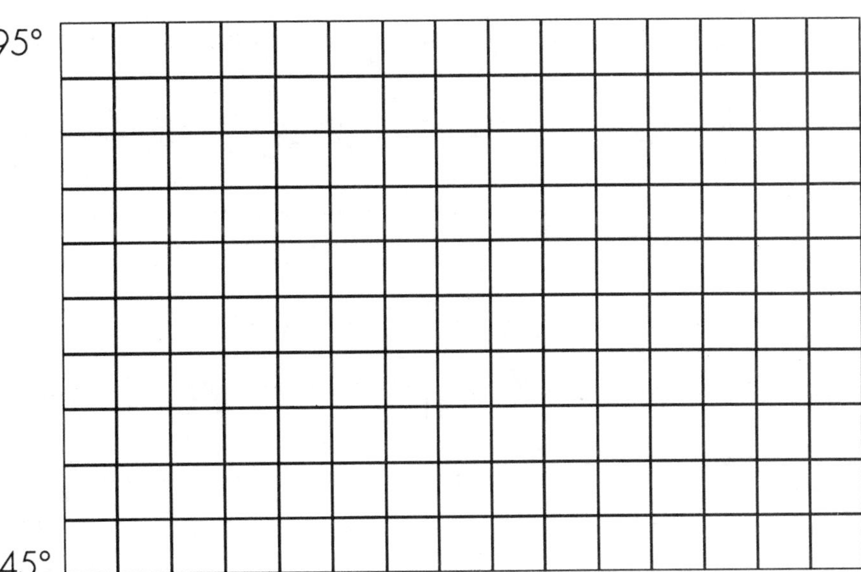

What is the average difference between the highs and lows for this week?

____

Look in a newspaper to try to find the city that shows the greatest difference between its high and low temperature. What is the city and what is the difference?

____

Name ______________________________

Magic Square 2

In a magic square, each row, column, and diagonal has the same sum. The magic square below has been started but not finished. Your task is to place numbers in the empty squares to finish the magic square. There is likely to be more than one way to finish the square. Just remember that each row, line, and diagonal must equal the same sum.

				Sum:
		6		____
7	6	9	13	____
	7			____
9	11			____

Sum: ____ ↙ ____ ____ ____ ____ ↘ ____

Name ______________________________

Tile Time

You are in charge of buying ceramic tiles for remodeling a bathroom. There are four walls that will be tiled. Each wall will have tile from the floor to a point measuring 46 ¾ inches from the floor.

The tiles are square, and each side measures 4 ¼".

Wall 1 is 17 inches wide. ______________________ tiles needed

Wall 2 is 93 ½ inches wide. ______________________ tiles needed

Wall 3 is 51 inches wide. ______________________ tiles needed

Wall 4 is 34 inches wide. ______________________ tiles needed

Total tiles needed for remodeling ______________________

There's a special price on these tiles this week. They cost 49¢ each.

What will be the total cost of the tiles? ______________________

Name ____________________

Brick Diamond

1995 brought the opening of Coors Field, a brand new ball park, in Denver, Colorado. Fans were given a chance to buy commemorative bricks which were laid out in the shape of a baseball diamond just outside the stadium.

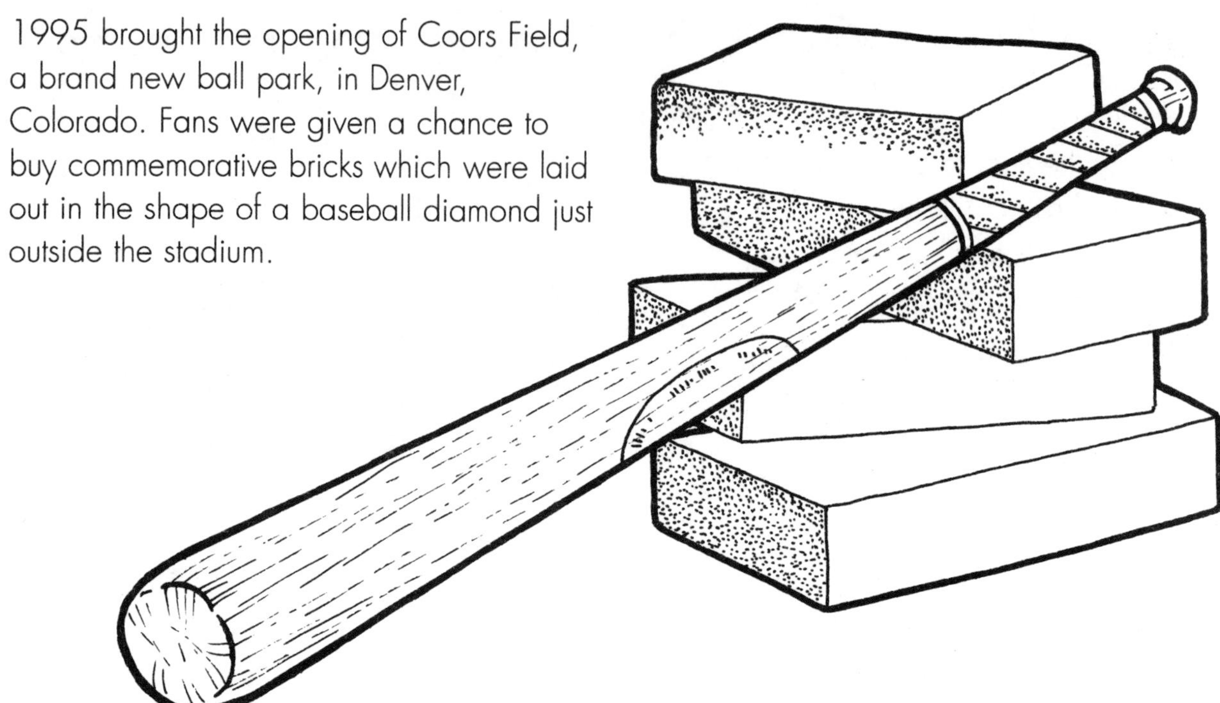

1. 8,576 commemorative bricks were sold for $75 each. What was the total amount of money raised by selling these bricks? ______________

2. Each of the bricks measures 4″ x 8″. How many square inches are on the side of each brick? ______________

3. What is the total surface area of all the bricks (only counting one side of each brick) in square inches? ______________

4. What is the approximate total surface area in square feet? ______________

5. Since the baseball diamond (the infield) is really a square, what is the approximate measurement in feet of each side of the brick baseball diamond?

____

Name ______________________

A Friendly Puzzle

Read each problem. Color in the answer on the hundred's chart.

1. Eleven pair
2. Two dozen
3. Ounces in two pounds + 2
4. One century – 14
5. 16¢ less than $1
6. Inches in two yards + 2
7. Players on four football teams
8. Eight squared
9. Inches in six feet
10. Sides on thirteen hexagons + 4
11. Sides on ten triangles + 2
12. Days in January and July
13. Players on six baseball teams
14. Three quarters + 1¢
15. Quarts in thirteen gallons
16. People in fourteen trios
17. Days in nine weeks + 3
18. Cups in fourteen quarts
19. Seven nickels + 1¢
20. Feet in seventeen yards + 2

1	2	3	4	5	6	7	8	9	10
11	12	13	14	15	16	17	18	19	20
21	22	23	24	25	26	27	28	29	30
31	32	33	34	35	36	37	38	39	40
41	42	43	44	45	46	47	48	49	50
51	52	53	54	55	56	57	58	59	60
61	62	63	64	65	66	67	68	69	70
71	72	73	74	75	76	77	78	79	80
81	82	83	84	85	86	87	88	89	90
91	92	93	94	95	96	97	98	99	100

Name ______________________

Change a Square

By moving only two circles, change this square into a triangle. You may cut out these circles to move around or use any other markers to help you. Actually, moving the markers around makes it easier to find a solution. Have fun!

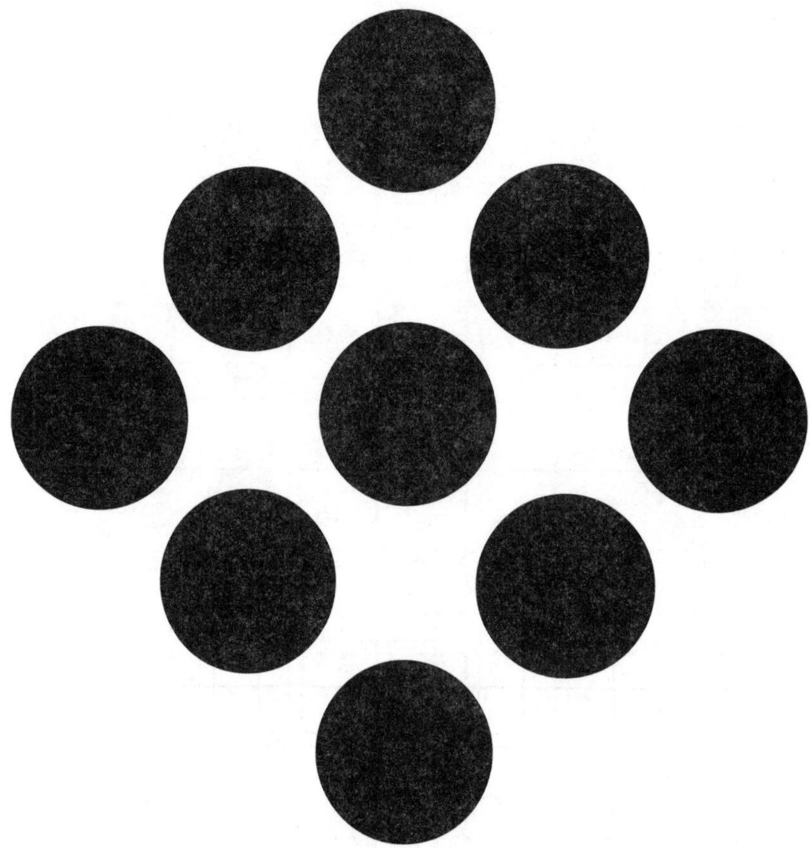

Name ______________________________

Draw 16

Draw four different figures, each having an area of 16 square units. Label each drawing. On the back of this paper, write your reasoning for each drawing that proves your drawing has an area of 16 square units.

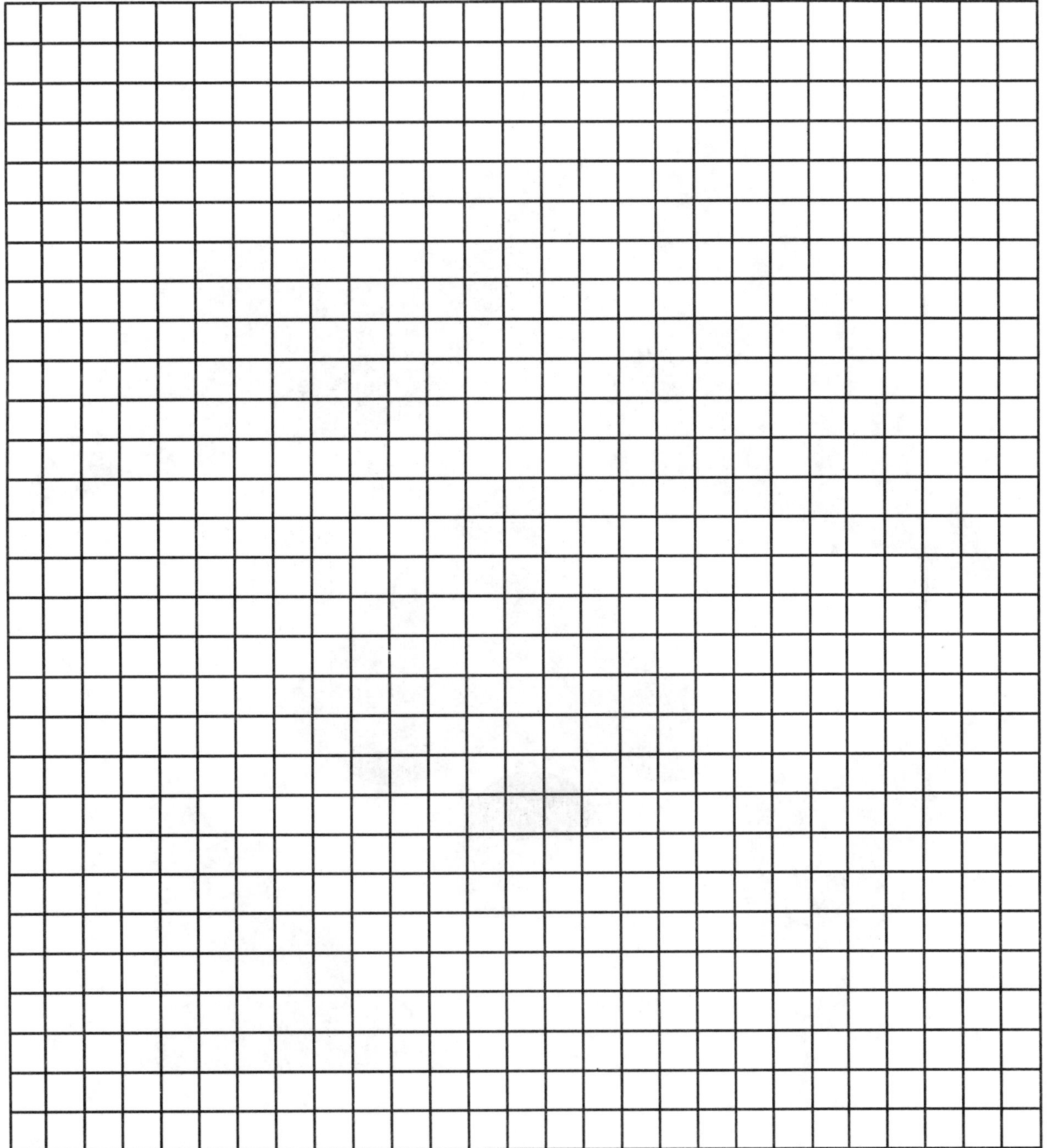

Name ______________________

Make a Square

Cut out the shapes on this page and put them together to make a square. While it is possible to make a square using only a few of the pieces, your challenge is to use all five pieces to make your square. Yes, it is possible!

Name ____________________

Figure the Area

The area for square F is 16 square units.

The area for square B is 25 square units.

The area for square H is 25 square units.

Find the area for the other squares.

Be ready to prove your answers.

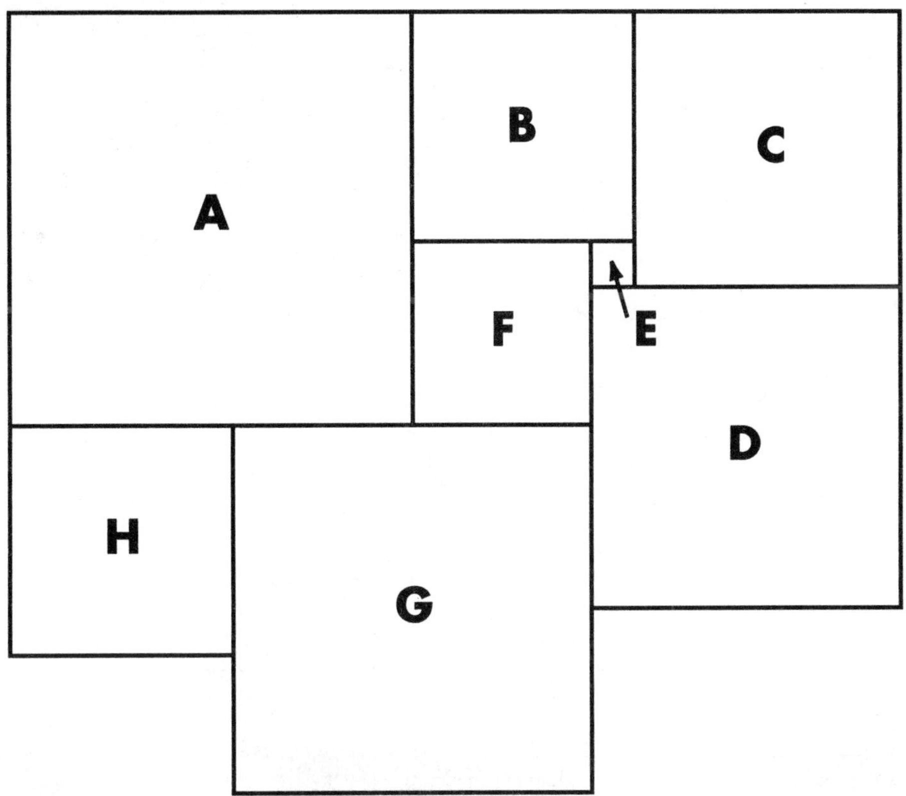

A = __________ square units

B = __________ square units

C = __________ square units

D = __________ square units

E = __________ square units

F = __________ square units

G = __________ square units

H = __________ square units

Name ______________________

Power Outage

After a recent storm, Katherine came home from work to find that the electricity had been off sometime during the day. The electric clock in the kitchen gave the time as 4:15. The digital clock on the bedroom clock radio, which resets to 12:00 when the electricity comes back on, gave the time as 6:20. The time on Katherine's wristwatch was 4:58.

1. How long was the electricity off? ______________________

2. What time did the electricity come back on? ______________________

3. What time did the electricity go off? ______________________

Explain how the above times were decided upon. ______________________

____

____

____

____

Name ______________________

Start With a Penny

It happened during the time when Sam had a month's vacation from school. His parents had many chores for him to do around the house and yard. His dad said that Sam would be paid for his work since his parents greatly valued Sam's help. As a matter of fact, Sam's dad offered to pay him $10 a day for 30 days' work. Sam thought about the offer and then made one of his own. Sam told his dad that he would be willing to work for pennies a day. He would work for 1¢ the first day, 2¢ the second day, 4¢ the third day, and so on with his pay doubling each day. For the 30 days, Sam would accept the amount he earned on the 30th day.

Circle the plan you think is the best.

Dad's Plan　　　　　　　　　　Sam's Plan

Find the exact dollar value of each plan.

Dad's plan for 30 days would be worth ______________________

Sam's plan for 30 days would be worth ______________________

Did you pick the best plan to begin with?

Name ______________________

Mystery Numbers

Are you number wise? Use the letters to help find what the number stands for. Numbers are all around us so you'll have to be alert and think hard.

Example:

365 = N of D in a Y

365 = Number of Days in a Year

1. 88 = K on a P ______________________
2. 12 = B on a P ______________________
3. 32 = D F at which W F ______________________
4. 5 = D in a Z C ______________________
5. 8 = S on a S S ______________________
6. 9 = I in a B G ______________________
7. 4 = Q in a D ______________________
8. 5280 = F in a M ______________________
9. 200 = D for P G in M ______________________
10. 100 = Y on a F F ______________________
11. 90 = F B B on a B F ______________________
12. 9 = P in the S S ______________________
13. 12 = E in a D ______________________
14. 360 = D in a C ______________________
15. 18 = H in G ______________________

Name ____________________

Tournament Planning

In many schools across the country, recreational sports tournaments are a common activity. Sometimes tournaments are planned for physical education classes, and many times they are part of after-school recreation programs. Having double elimination tournaments means that all teams get to play at least two games instead of being eliminated after their first loss. This allows for more participation which is usually one of the tournament goals.

Below is a model of the bracketing used for a double elimination tournament with four teams. On another piece of paper, draw the bracketing that would be used for a double elimination tournament involving eight teams.

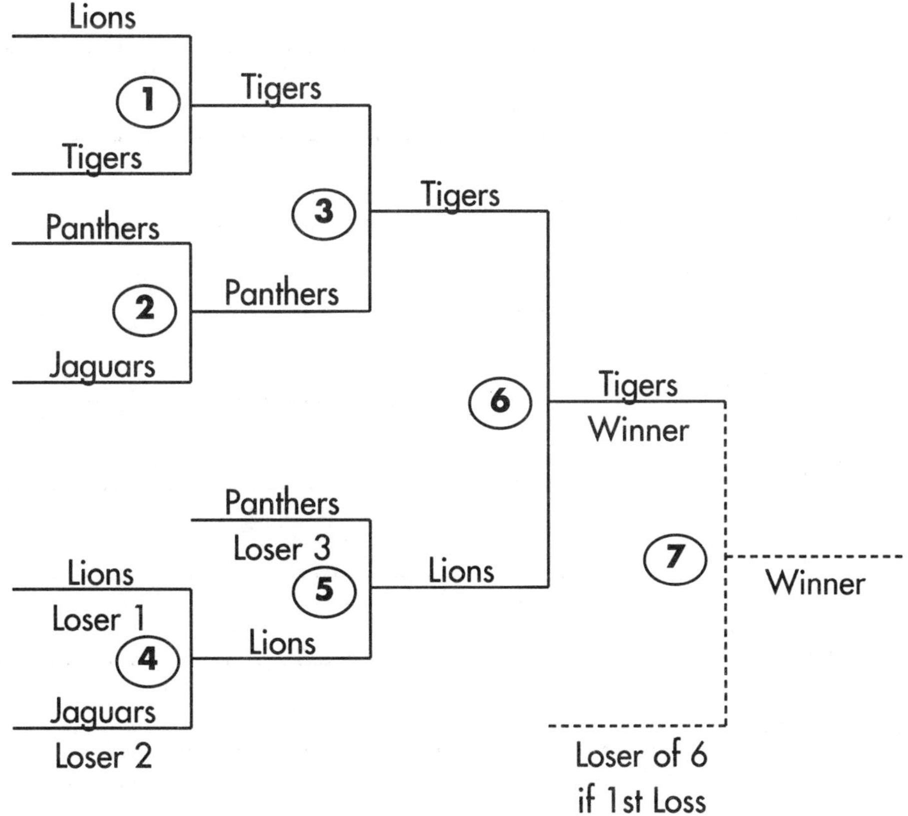

Name ______________________

Give Me the Odds

The objective of this activity is to find the sum of the first 25 odd counting numbers. One way is to add 1 + 3 + 5 continuing until you have added the first 25 odd numbers to find the answer. However, this is too much work for this problem. Look for patterns and combinations to find a much shorter and easier way to solve this problem. Try to work smarter, not longer.

Answer = ______________

Now that you have found the answer to the sum of the first 25 odd counting numbers, apply what you have learned and find the sum of the first 25 even counting numbers.

Answer = ______________

Name ______________________

Windchill Factor

The windchill factor is a measure of what cold weather feels like to the average person depending on the combination of the temperature and the wind. When the apparent or "feels like" temperature reaches freezing, the danger of frostbite can begin. The lower the "feels like" temperature goes, the greater the danger of frostbite. Shade in the boxes for freezing and below freezing conditions using a color or pattern to identify them. Do not cover the number that indicates the windchill temperature.

Air Temperature (°F)	Wind speed in miles per hour								
	0	5	10	15	20	25	30	35	40
	Apparent or "Feels Like" Temperature								
35	35	32	22	16	12	8	6	4	3
30	30	27	16	9	4	1	2	-4	-5
25	25	22	10	2	-3	-7	-10	-12	-13
20	20	16	3	-5	-10	-15	-18	-20	-21
15	15	11	-3	-11	-17	-22	-25	-27	-29
10	10	6	-9	-18	-24	-29	-33	-35	-37
5	5	0	-15	-25	-31	-36	-41	-43	-45
0	0	-5	-22	-31	-39	-44	-49	-52	-53
-5	-5	-10	-27	-38	-46	-51	-56	-58	-60
-10	-10	-15	-34	-45	-53	-59	-64	-67	-69
-15	-15	-21	-40	-51	-60	-66	-71	-74	-76
-20	-20	-26	-46	-58	-67	-74	-79	-82	-84
-25	-25	-31	-52	-65	-74	-81	-86	-89	-92

Find the highest temperature on the chart at which freezing conditions are possible.

____

Find the lowest wind speed on the chart at which freezing conditions are possible.

____

How common are these air temperatures and wind speeds in your area? __________

Name ______________________________

Graph It Smaller

Draw the hidden picture in the graph. First, pick any puzzle piece. Next, find the correct location for it on the grid by using the letter and number that identify it. Last, draw the piece in its correct location. Hint: The graph is smaller than the puzzle pieces. Some squares on the grid do not have a puzzle piece. This means the square is all white.

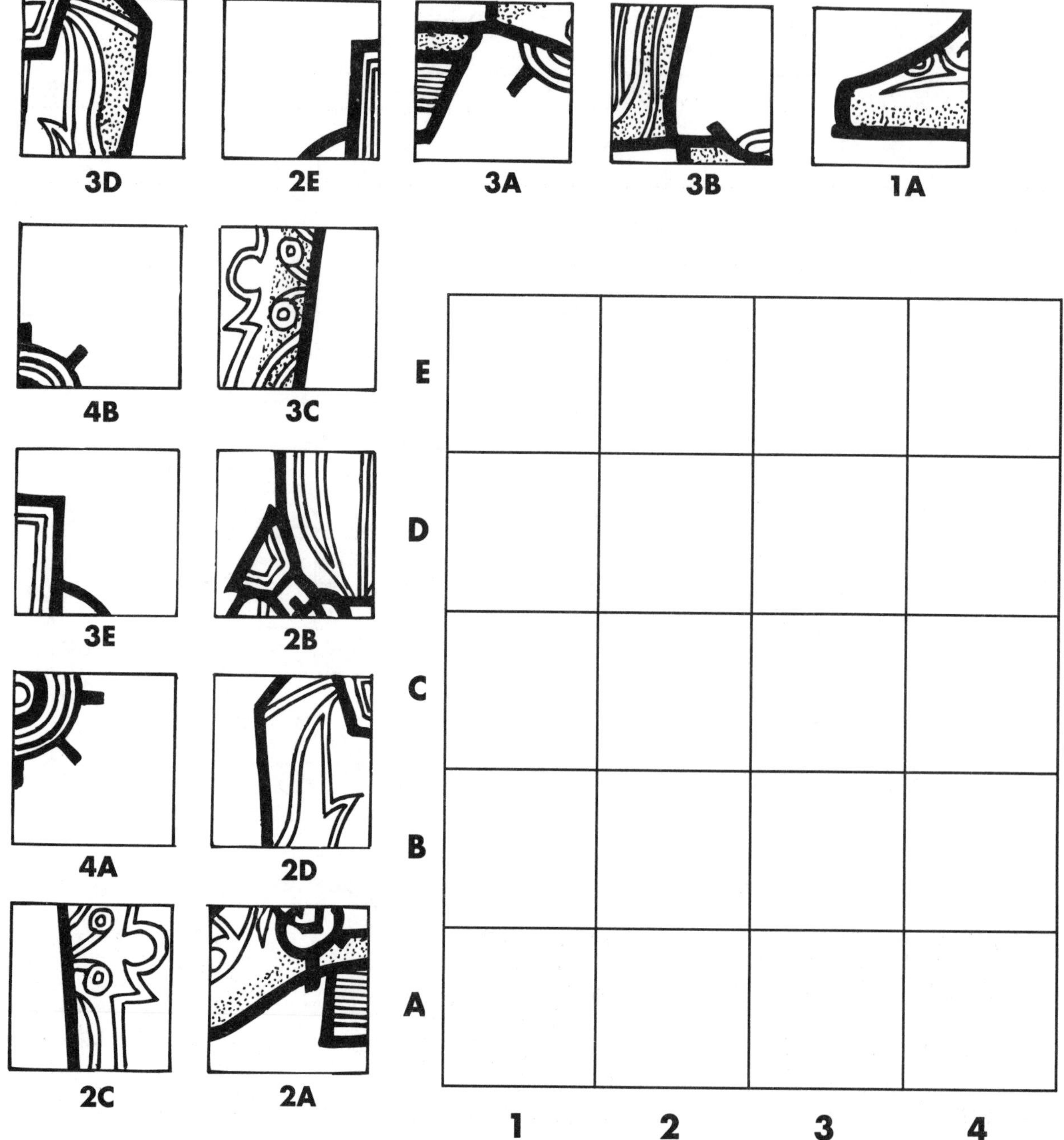

Name ______________________

Combination Count

1 2 3 4 5 6 7 8 9

How many different 2-digit numbers can be made using the counting numbers 1 to 9?

____

How did you arrive at your answer? ______________________

____

____

Name ______________________

Post Time

Roger has been after his parents for some time to let him have a dog. Finally they said he could have a dog on two conditions. The first condition is that Roger fence in an area for the dog so that it has a secure place to stay when Roger is at school. There is some fencing out back that Roger can use, but the fence posts will have to be purchased to enclose the area. The second condition is that although Roger won't have to pay for the fence posts, he must figure out exactly how much the posts will cost. This way, his parents will know how much money to allow for this project.

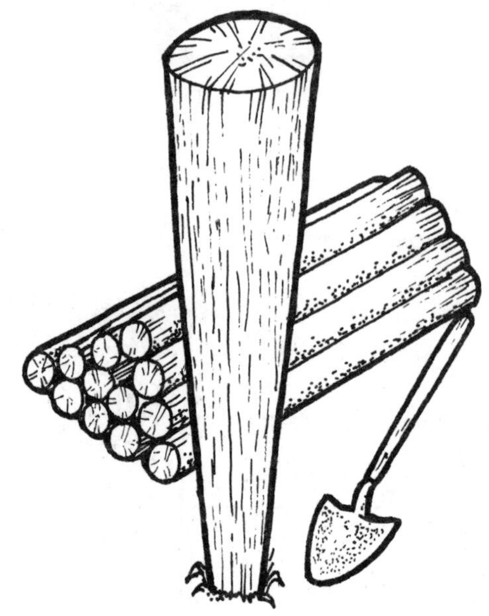

Roger measured the area for the dog. He found the dimensions to be 21 feet by 17.5 feet. Roger's dad explained to him that the fence posts must be put in every 3½ feet. Each fence post costs $5.25.

1. How many fence posts will Roger need? __________

2. How much money will Roger's parents need for the fence posts? __________

Name ______________________

Make a Rectangle

Cut out the shapes on this page and put them together to make a rectangle that's not a square. While it is possible to make a rectangle using only a few of the pieces, your challenge is to use all six pieces to make your rectangle. Yes, it's possible.

Name ____________________

Shelly's French Fries

Shelly is the co-owner of a restaurant that is known for selling large orders of curly French fries. On a busy summer day, the restaurant uses 300-400 pounds of potatoes for these very popular fries. The restaurant is only open Monday - Friday.

1. Approximately how many potatoes would there be in 400 pounds of potatoes? Hint: There are about 20 potatoes in a 5-pound sack of potatoes. ____________

2. The restaurant uses about two potatoes per order of French fries. How many orders of French fries would be made on a day when 400 pounds of potatoes are used? ____________

3. If the delivery truck brings one half ton of potatoes every Wednesday and Friday, how many pounds of potatoes are delivered each week? ____________

4. How many pounds of potatoes are delivered each year? ____________

5. The restaurant makes approximately how many orders of French fries per week? (Remember: The restaurant is only open Monday - Friday.) ____________

6. The restaurant makes approximately how many orders of French fries per year? ____________

7. If potatoes cost $8 per 50 pounds, what is the cost of potatoes for each week? ____________________

8. What is the cost of potatoes for the year? ____________________

9. During June, July, and August, the cost of the potatoes goes up to $11 per 50 pounds. This is because the new potatoes haven't been harvested yet, and the potatoes must come from the warehouse which has higher prices. Adjust the yearly cost of the potatoes to reflect this increase in cost. ____________________

Name ______________________

How Many Miles?

Although the car advertisement claimed that the car would get a certain amount of miles for each gallon of gas, George wanted to find out for himself what his car would get. Figuring m.p.g. (miles per gallon) is simple. Just subtract the mileage of the last time the car was filled with gas from the mileage the current time the car is filled with gas. Then divide the mileage by the number of gallons of gas put in the car. The result is the m.p.g.

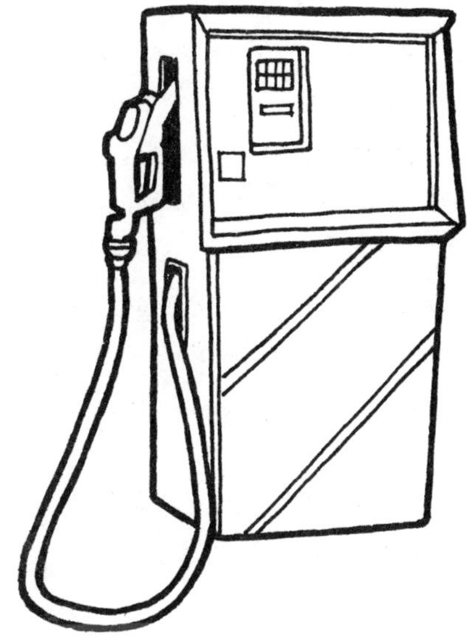

Example:

Current gas fill up		37594.1
Last gas fill up	−	37316.2
		277.9

Divide 277.9 miles by 10.6 (the gallons of gas needed to fill up the tank).

277.9 ÷ 10.6 = 26.2 miles per gallon

Find the following miles per gallon.

Starting mileage: 41455.8

1. 41798.7 — 12 gal — miles per gallon ____________
2. 42036.2 — 8.7 gal — miles per gallon ____________
3. 42262.2 — 7.6 gal — miles per gallon ____________
4. 42476.8 — 6.8 gal — miles per gallon ____________
5. 42690.7 — 7.1 gal — miles per gallon ____________
6. 42920.0 — 8.1 gal — miles per gallon ____________
7. 43235.9 — 13.5 gal — miles per gallon ____________
8. What is the average miles per gallon for this time period? ____________

Name ______________________

Don't Touch!

Cut out the puzzle pieces at the bottom of the page. Then arrange them on the empty circles in the triangle so that no identical pieces touch each other. When you have the solution, either glue or tape the pieces in place.

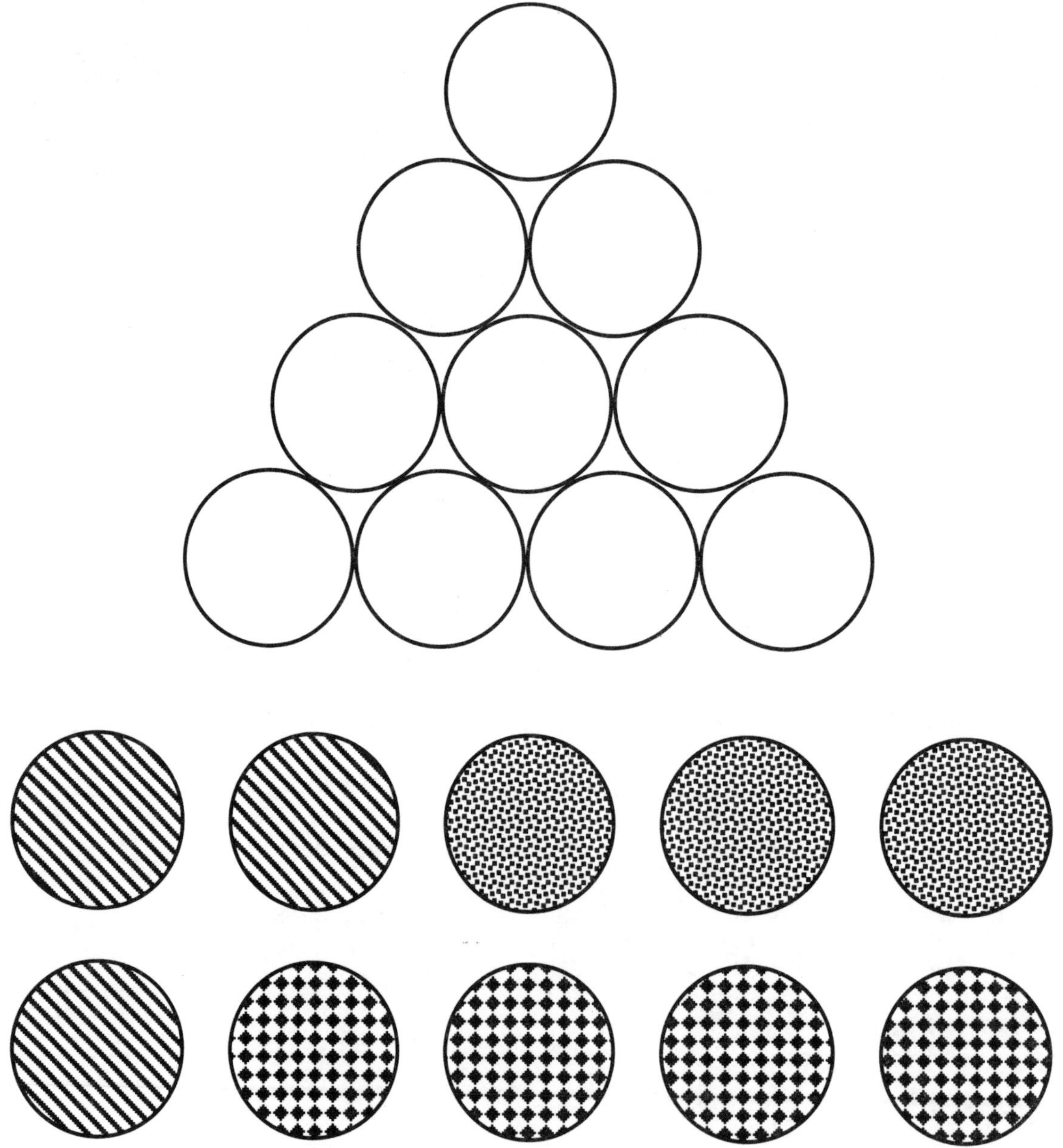

Name ____________________

Choose Your Pay

A new company in town has just posted a job vacancy and is looking for someone with some math sense and problem-solving ability. You are one of two finalists for the position. During your final interview with the president of the company, the last question you are asked is about the salary you would prefer. You have two choices. The first choice is a salary of $25,000 with a raise of $1000 at the end of each year. The second choice is a salary of $12,500 for each half of the year with a raise of $250 at the end of each half year. The company president has made it clear that the person who has the math sense to choose the salary that will have paid the most after the first five years will get the job. It's up to you now!

Choice 1

Year	Amount
Year 1	________
Year 2	________
Year 3	________
Year 4	________
Year 5	________

Choice 2

Year	Amount
Year 1	________
Year 2	________
Year 3	________
Year 4	________
Year 5	________

Which choice will you make? ____________________

How much more will your choice have paid after five years? ________

Explain how you arrived at your answers.

Name______________________

Geometry Vocabulary

Find and circle the geometry vocabulary words in the chart below.

H	C	Q	O	P	T	N	E	U	R	G	N	O	C	C
W	E	I	U	V	N	O	G	A	T	C	O	R	U	C
L	D	X	R	A	A	B	D	K	Y	V	A	R	O	P
L	O	S	A	C	D	L	L	Z	G	L	V	N	E	A
A	D	Y	H	G	L	R	W	J	U	E	E	U	L	R
T	E	M	E	V	O	E	I	C	C	P	D	G	G	A
N	C	M	V	A	M	N	I	L	D	I	R	L	N	L
O	A	E	C	T	D	D	R	N	A	B	J	N	A	L
Z	G	T	Z	V	N	E	H	N	O	T	M	N	I	E
I	O	R	L	E	D	S	O	D	P	G	E	O	R	L
R	N	Y	P	N	Q	N	O	F	Y	R	A	R	T	H
O	R	R	I	U	A	N	T	B	F	D	I	C	A	P
H	E	L	A	G	P	Y	R	A	M	I	D	S	E	L
P	Y	R	O	P	E	N	T	A	G	O	N	G	M	D
C	E	N	N	O	I	T	A	L	L	E	S	S	E	T

circle
cone
congruent
curve
cylinder
decagon
dodecagon
hexagon
horizontal
nonagon
octagon
oval
parallel
pentagon
perpendicular
prism
pyramid
quadrilateral
square
symmetry
tessellation
triangle

Name ____________________

No Word Problems

Some students do not like to solve word problems. So just for those students, here are some problems with the words left out! You will have to fill in just a few words to solve these problems. Write the problem and its answer on the line.

1. 8D – 24H = 1W ____________________
2. 4P = 8 ____________________
3. 104Y – 4Y = 1C ____________________
4. S – 7 = Z ____________________
5. 2P = 1Q ____________________
6. S R of 4 = T ____________________
7. 1 + 3Z = 1T ____________________
8. P & N & D & Q & H D are all C ____________________

    ____
9. F x T = E ____________________
10. 1D + 1D = 1S ____________________
11. 60S + 60S = 2M ____________________
12. 1H ÷ F = T ____________________
13. 3 B M + 3 L P = 6A ____________________
14. T x T = 1H ____________________
15. O + T + T + F = T ____________________

Name ____________________

Palindromes

Palindromes are words, phrases, or numbers that are the same whether they are read forward or backward. Number palindromes are easy to make. Example:

Original number	463
Reverse the number and add.	+364
	827
Reverse again and add.	+728
	1555
Reverse again and add.	+5551
	7106
Reverse again and add.	+6017
	13123
Reverse again and add.	+32131
A palindrome!	45254

This is a five-step palindrome because there were five numbers added. Use scratch paper to find palindromes with different numbers of steps. You can count the number of + signs or the number of new answers to determine the number of steps. Find as many as you can.

3-step numbers	4-step numbers	5-step numbers
________	________	________
________	________	________
________	________	________

6-step numbers	7-step numbers	More?
________	________	________
________	________	________

Name ______________________________

Even Money

Cut out the coins at the bottom of the page. Then arrange them on the grid so that the value of the circles is the same in any line, row, and corner-to-corner diagonal. When you have the solution, either glue or tape the coins in place.

Name ____________________

The Recording Industry

The United States recording industry has been selling millions of recordings for many years. Over the 15-year period from 1975 to 1990, the type of recordings sold changed dramatically as shown by the figures below. Fill in the blanks for total sales for each year and the percentage of sales for each category change. Round the percentages to the nearest tenth.

1975	Total Sales ________		
Singles	Albums LP/EP	Compact Discs	Cassettes
164,000,000	257,000,000	0	16,200,000
% of total____	% of total____	% of total____	% of total____

1980	Total Sales ________		
Singles	Albums LP/EP	Compact Discs	Cassettes
164,300,000	322,800,000	0	110,200,000
% of total____	% of total____	% of total____	% of total____

1985	Total Sales ________		
Singles	Albums LP/EP	Compact Discs	Cassettes
120,700,000	167,000,000	22,600,000	339,100,000
% of total____	% of total____	% of total____	% of total____

1990	Total Sales ________		
Singles	Albums LP/EP	Compact Discs	Cassettes
27,600,000	11,700,000	286,500,000	442,200,000
% of total____	% of total____	% of total____	% of total____

Name ______________________

Receiving Change

Spending money is an activity that many of us do fairly frequently. When a purchase is made, change is received and put away. Often change is given all at once instead of being counted. You must be able to look at change quickly and know if it is correct. Can you do that?

For each purchase listed, give the amount of change due and list the bills and coins needed to make the change.

1. Purchase amount: $4.17 Cash received: $5 Change owed __________

   bills and coins in change ______________________________

2. Purchase amount: $7.38 Cash received: $10 Change owed __________

   bills and coins in change ______________________________

3. Purchase amount: $8.23 Cash received: $10 Change owed __________

   bills and coins in change ______________________________

4. Purchase amount: $16.39 Cash received: $20 Change owed __________

   bills and coins in change ______________________________

5. Purchase amount: $4.06 Cash received: $5 Change owed __________

   bills and coins in change ______________________________

Name ______________________________

Working Together

House painting is a big job. Jerry found that out after he had painted several houses by himself. Although he could paint a house in six days, he wanted to get the houses painted in a shorter length of time so his painting business could get more contracts. Jerry hired Jeff to help him because Jeff could paint a house in four days.

How many days did it take Jerry and Jeff to paint a house when they worked together?

____

Explain how you arrived at your answer.

Name ______________________________

Heat Index

The heat index is a measure of what hot weather feels like to the average person depending on the combination of the temperature and the humidity. When the apparent or "feels like" temperature reaches 105° or more, sunstroke and heat exhaustion are likely. Shade in the "feels like" boxes for these conditions using a color or pattern to identify them. Do not cover the number that indicates the heat index temperature.

What is the lowest temperature and lowest humidity at which sunstroke and heat exhaustion are possible?

1. Temperature __________ 2. Humidity __________

When the apparent or "feels like" temperature reaches 90°, heat exhaustion is possible. Shade in the "feels like" boxes that indicate that heat exhaustion is possible using a different color or pattern to identify them. Do not cover the number that indicates the heat index temperature.

What is the lowest temperature and lowest humidity at which heat exhaustion is possible?

3. Temperature __________ 4. Humidity __________

Air Temperature

Apparent or "Feels Like" Temperature

Relative Humidity	**75°**	**80°**	**85°**	**90°**	**95°**	**100°**	**105°**	**110°**	**115°**	**120°**
0%	69	73	78	83	87	91	95	99	103	107
10%	70	75	80	85	90	95	100	105	111	116
20%	72	77	82	87	93	99	105	112	120	130
30%	73	78	84	90	96	104	113	123	135	148
40%	74	79	86	93	101	110	123	137	151	
50%	75	81	88	96	107	120	135	150		
60%	76	82	90	100	114	132	149			
70%	77	85	93	106	124	144				
80%	78	86	97	113	136					
90%	79	88	102	122						
100%	80	91	108							

How common are these air temperatures and humidity levels in your area?

Name ______________________________

Square Where?

Look carefully at the figure below. It was made by overlapping six squares.

1. Cut out the six squares at the bottom of the page and duplicate the figure.
2. On the original figure, place a 1 on the square that is the first one you put down, 2 on the second square you placed in the design, 3 on the third square you placed in the design and continue until 6 is on the last square placed in the design.

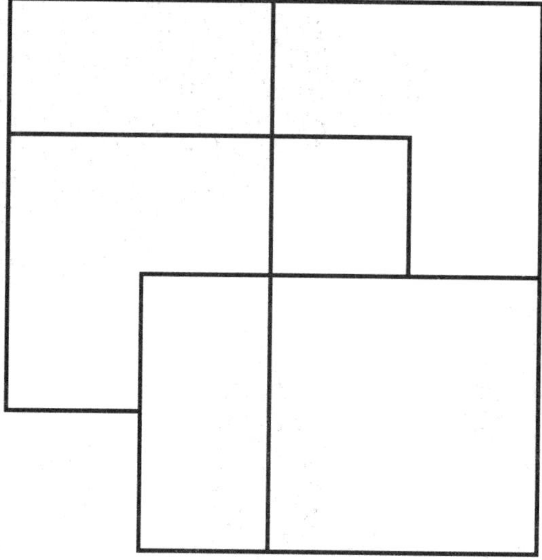

Name ______________________________

Make a Trapezoid

Cut out the shapes on this page and put them together to make a trapezoid. Remember: A trapezoid must have four sides with two of the sides being parallel. All of the six pieces must be used.

Name ______________________________

Do I Use It?

Of course mathematics is useful in math class! It also would be useful to a banker and an accountant. How about in our everyday lives? Is math at all useful to you? Think about that carefully. Remember that math is not just problems with numbers in them. Geometry, probability, estimation, and a variety of measurements are some areas of math that might be useful to you. See how long a list you can make of the ways you use mathematics just for today. Then, expand your list to include other days of this week. The possibilities may surprise you!

Today	Other Days
______________________________	______________________________
______________________________	______________________________
______________________________	______________________________
______________________________	______________________________
______________________________	______________________________
______________________________	______________________________
______________________________	______________________________
______________________________	______________________________
______________________________	______________________________
______________________________	______________________________
______________________________	______________________________
______________________________	______________________________
______________________________	______________________________

Name ____________________

Television Ratings

Here are the prime-time television ratings for one week in July. One rating point equals 954,000 television households. How many households were watching each program? Round your answers to the nearest 100,000.

Top 10

1.	NBC	Rating 15.8	Homes ____________
2.	NBC	Rating 14.3	Homes ____________
3.	ABC	Rating 13.9	Homes ____________
4.	NBC	Rating 13.7	Homes ____________
5.	ABC	Rating 12.6	Homes ____________
6.	ABC	Rating 12.0	Homes ____________
7.	(tie) ABC	Rating 11.9	Homes ____________
7.	(tie) NBC	Rating 11.9	Homes ____________
9.	CBS	Rating 11.6	Homes ____________
10.	(tie) ABC	Rating 11.5	Homes ____________
10.	(tie) CBS	Rating 11.5	Homes ____________

What is the average rating for each network and the average number of homes watching that network?

ABC Rating ________ Homes ____________

CBS Rating ________ Homes ____________

NBC Rating ________ Homes ____________

Name ________________________________

Line Layout

Using a straight-edge, draw all the line segments listed below. You may wish to "jazz up" this design when you are finished!

H3	X1	MY	XO	P1	IS	DE	CX
CD	QA	AP	BC	X2	MN	JI	XG
J3	4Z	X3	GH	FE	OP	1B	RE
ZM	XK	F2	X4	AB	A1	D2	E2
NO	N4	I3	ZK	M4	FG	HI	JK

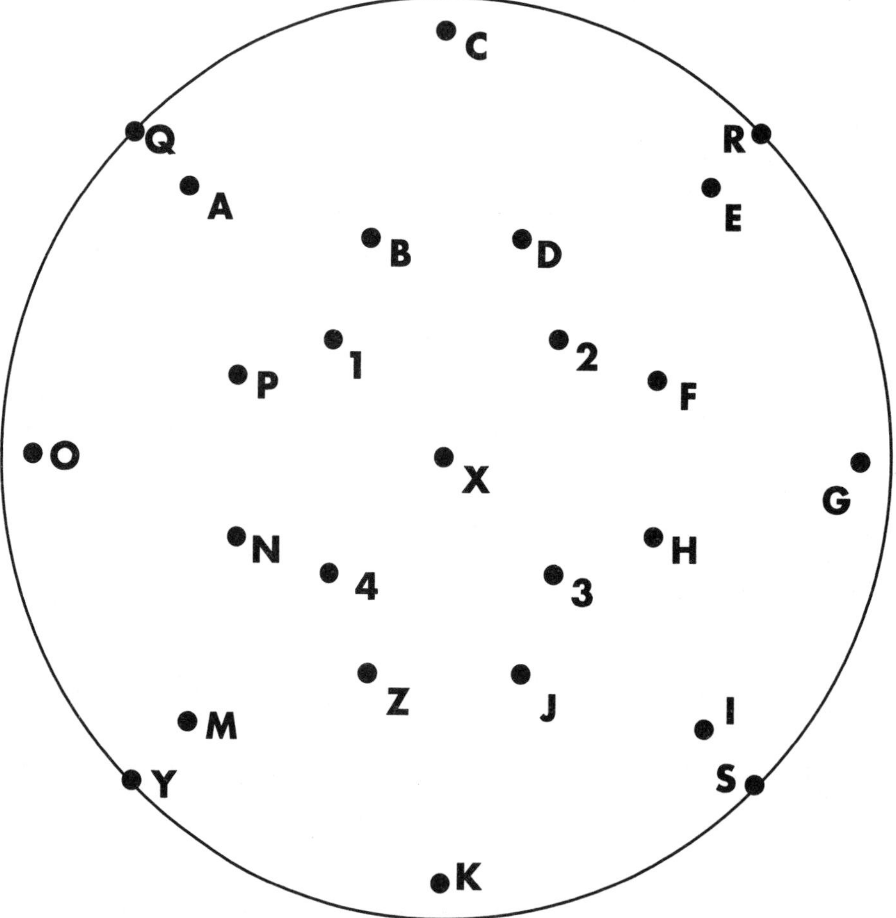

Try your hand at making a different line layout on the back of this paper or on another sheet of paper. Give it to a classmate to solve.

Name ______________________________

Buy a Pass

If you go swimming at the city pool, you will see the following sign posted.

Daily Swim Fees	
13-and-over:	$2.00
12-and-under:	$1.25

It is not always convenient to come to the swimming pool with the exact amount of money for swimming. Also, the management feels that if someone comes swimming often, that person should get a break on the price. With those thoughts in mind, the management has decided to offer a 20-punch swim card that will cost the swimmer 15% less than the amount needed to buy 20 individual tickets.

1. What will the 13-and-over 20-punch card cost? ______________

2. What is the per-swim price using this 20-punch card? ______________

3. What will the 12-and-under 20-punch card cost? ______________

4. What is the per-swim price using this 20-punch card? ______________

If the 20-punch card is well received, a 30-punch swim card that gives the buyer a 20% savings over the individual ticket cost will be introduced.

5. What will the 13-and-over 30-punch card cost? ______________

6. What is the per-swim price using this 30-punch card? ______________

7. What will the 12-and-under 30-punch card cost? ______________

8. What is the per-swim price using this 30-punch card? ______________

Name ______________________________

Find Their Places

Cut out the puzzle pieces at the bottom of the page. Then arrange them on the empty grid so that there are no two identical pieces in any line, row, or diagonal. When you have the solution, either glue or tape the pieces in place.

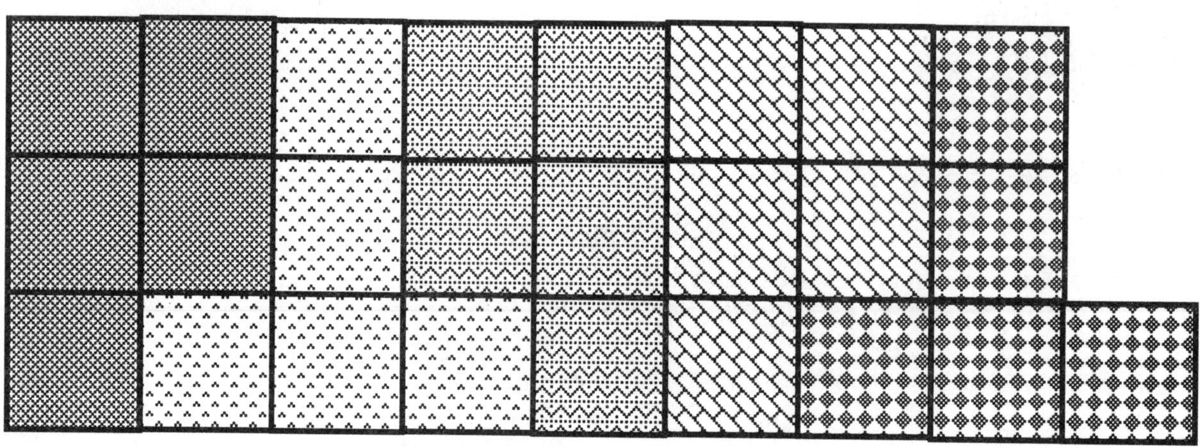

Name ____________________

Rectangle/Triangle

Cut out the shapes on this page and put them together to make a rectangle. You must use all five pieces in your rectangle. Then, rearrange the five pieces to make a triangle. Be prepared to show your teacher how you arranged the pieces to make each shape. You might want to draw diagrams to help you remember.

Name ____________________

Tony's Commercials

Tony is an actor living in New York City. In addition to acting in the theater, he also does commercials that are shown on national television. Of course, it's exciting to see Tony on television! We also know that the more we see him, the better it is for him. Why? Because there is a pay rate set by Actor's Equity for commercials airing on national television. The rate is based on the number of times the commercial is shown in a 13-week period.

National Commercial Pay Scale

The day of shooting and the first showing = $444
Showing 2 through showing 9 = $300 each
Showing 10 through showing 20 = $150 each
More than 20 showings = $75 each
At the end of 13 weeks, the rate starts over
with showings 1 through 9 at $300 each, etc.

1. If one of Tony's commercials is shown 25 times in a 13-week period, how much money will he make? ____________________

2. If Tony's commercial is only shown 13 times in a 13-week period, how much money will he make? ____________________

3. If Tony shoots a commercial on January 2 and it is then shown 2 times a week for the whole year, how much money will he make for the year?

   ____

4. A commercial is shot and is going to be shown for 13 weeks. How many times must it air for the actor to earn $500 a week? ____________________

5. One year, an actor earned $20,976 from commercials. Each 13-week period, he filmed a new commercial. Each 13-week period had the same number of showings. How many times was the commercial shown each 13-week period?

   ____

Name ______________________________

Howard the Humongous

Howard the Humongous is a very large and strong pack mule. A local farmer is planning to use Howard to carry his crop of carrots to market. The farmer has 3,000 carrots. The market is 1,000 miles away. Howard can only carry 1,000 carrots at one time. Unfortunately, Howard eats one carrot for every mile he walks. This trip is going to need some real planning. What is the largest number of carrots that the farmer can expect to get to the market? Be ready to explain how you arrived at your answer.

Name____________________

Multiply Odd

Circle the pairs of adjacent numbers in the rows below whose product is odd when they are multiplied. For example, in row one, 5 and 6 should not be circled as their product is even. Six and 8 should not be circled either as well as 6 and 7. But, 7 and 3 should be circled because their product is odd.

5 6 8 6 7 3 2 4 7 5 6 8 9 1 7 3 4 5 6 5

4 2 3 4 5 3 7 4 7 2 8 4 7 5 6 3 4 5 8 6

4 5 4 2 8 7 5 4 6 3 2 2 5 6 1 9 7 3 1 1

7 2 6 4 2 3 8 9 4 3 4 8 3 5 4 6 1 8 6 7

9 5 7 6 4 9 4 2 5 8 3 7 9 3 5 6 7 6 9 4

3 3 3 6 7 8 5 4 4 1 2 3 4 3 6 7 8 5 3 4

9 5 2 4 8 5 4 3 5 9 8 4 5 8 2 3 1 5 8 8

5 1 5 4 4 9 4 5 6 6 8 5 3 4 9 5 2 4 8 5

4 3 5 9 8 4 5 8 2 3 5 8 8 5 1 5 4 7 7 6

6 6 7 3 5 8 5 5 3 4 9 9 9 4 7 6 6 7 2 5

6 2 7 9 6 1 2 3 4 5 6 7 8 9 7 6 4 4 3 2

Is there a pattern? ____

____

Name________________________________

Figure It Out

To solve the puzzle below, choose a number from 1 to 9 to put in the empty squares. The three rows across and the three columns down must be correct number sentences. Some numbers may be used more than once, and other numbers may not be used. The calculations must be performed in the order given.

	x		–	6	= 9
+		+		–	
	+	1	–		= 2
÷		+		–	
2	x		+		= 7
= 5		= 7		= 1	

Name ____________________

How Many Squares?

How many squares can you find in the figure on this page? Count carefully!

Number of Squares ________

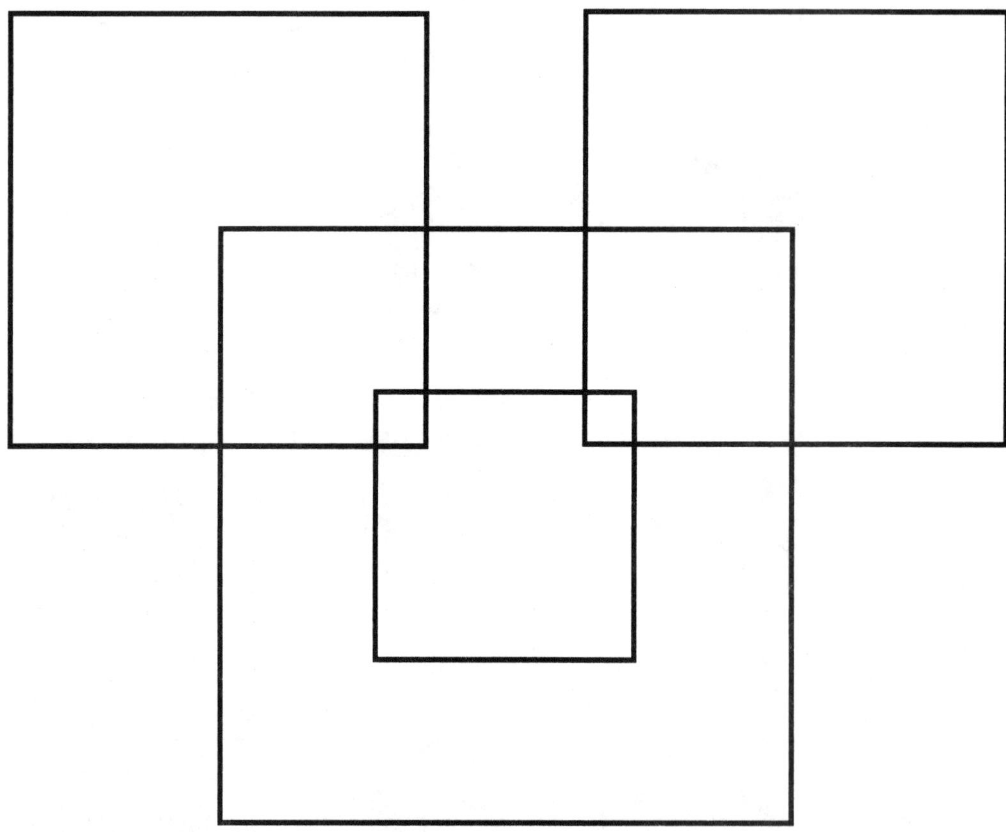

Name ____________________

Show One Half

Color each of the squares below so that exactly one half of the area is colored and exactly one half of the area is white. Color each square so that even if the figure is flipped or rotated, it is still unlike any other colored shape you have.

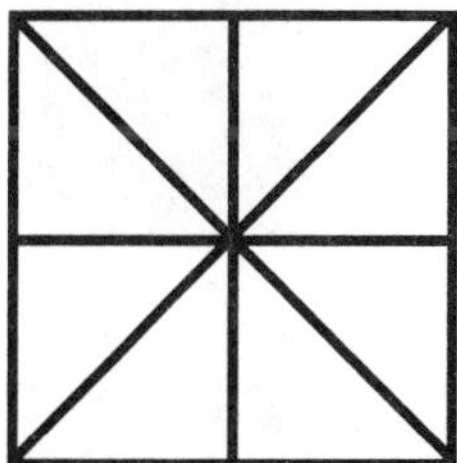
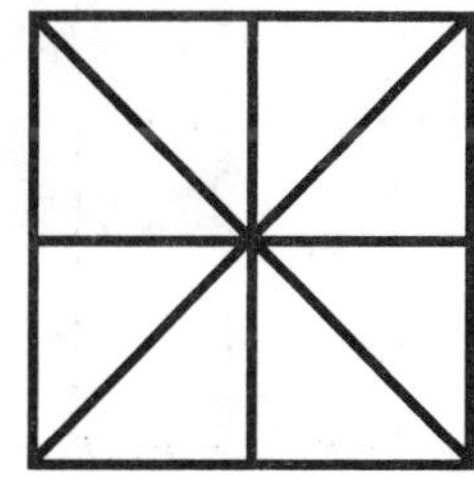
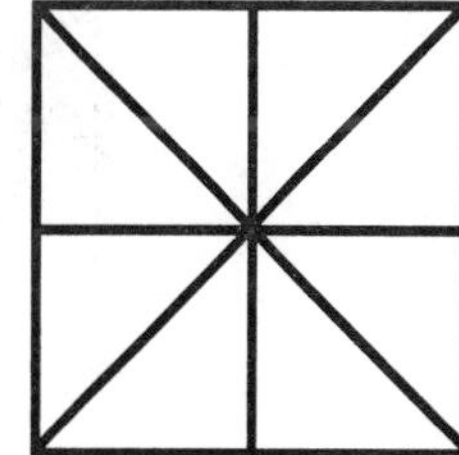

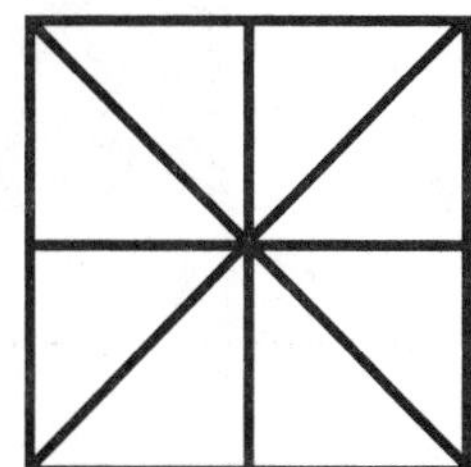

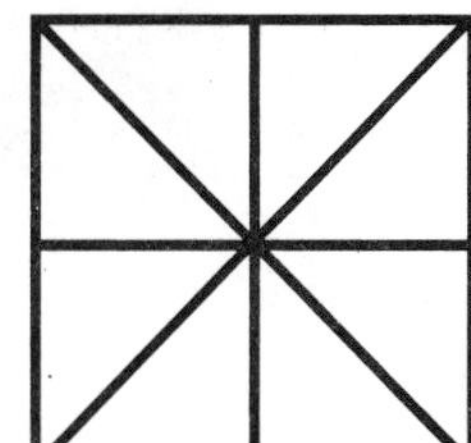
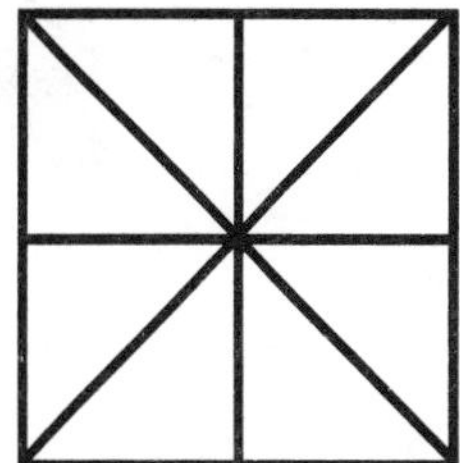

Name________________________________

Another Figure It Out!

To solve the puzzle below, choose a number from 1 to 9 to put in the empty squares. The three rows across and the three columns down must be correct number sentences. Some numbers may be used more than once, and other numbers may not be used. The calculations must be performed in the order given.

	x		÷		= 2
–		+		–	
	+	5	–	1	= 6
+		–		–	
	+		–		= 5
= 7		= 7		= 3	

Name ____________________

Paint Power

Jenny has decided to paint her bedroom. In order to know how much paint to buy, she got out her yardstick to measure her room. Two of the walls are 10 feet wide and 7 ½ feet high. The other two walls are 12 feet wide and 7 ½ feet high. The ceiling is 10 feet by 12 feet. Two areas won't need to be painted—two doorways each measuring 3 feet by 7 feet, and three windows each measuring 3 feet wide and 4 ½ feet high.

1. What is the total area that will be painted? ____________________

2. The label on the paint can says that one gallon will cover about 400 square feet. If this is true, then one quart will probably cover 100 square feet. How much paint should Jenny buy if she paints everything the same color? ____________________

3. If Jenny paints the walls one color and the ceiling another color, how much paint should she buy for each color?

   Ceiling ____________________ Walls ____________________

4. The ad in Sunday's newspaper had paint that regularly cost $16.97 a gallon on sale for $12.99 a gallon. What percent discount is this? ____________________

5. With the sale paint at $12.99 a gallon and $3.56 per quart, how much will the paint cost if Jenny uses just one color? ____________________

6. How much will the paint cost if she uses one color for the ceiling and another for the walls? ____________________

Name ____________________

How Many Triangles?

How many triangles can you find in the figure on this page? Count carefully!

Number of Triangles ________

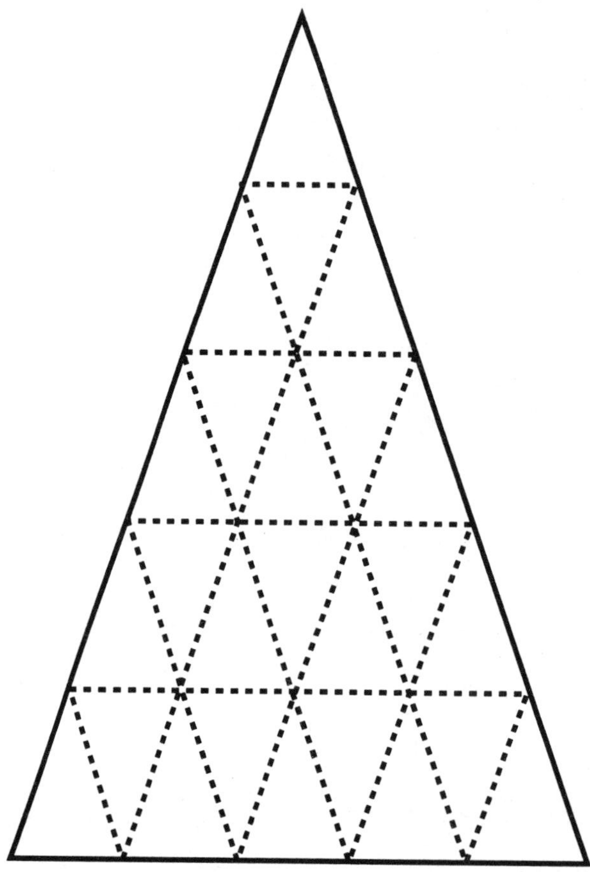

Name ____________________

Flight Time

The airline schedule from Cleveland, OH, to Colorado Springs, CO, gives the following timetable:

	Leaves Cleveland	Arrives in Colorado Springs
1.	6:55 a.m.	9:16 a.m.
2.	8:55 a.m.	12:20 p.m.
3.	11:15 a.m.	2:27 p.m.
4.	2:05 p.m.	5:42 p.m.
5.	6:04 p.m.	8:31 p.m.

Without counting the hours gained or lost by time zone changes, which flight takes the least time in actual transit according to this schedule?

____

Without counting the hours gained or lost by time zone changes, which flight takes the most time in actual transit according to this schedule?

____

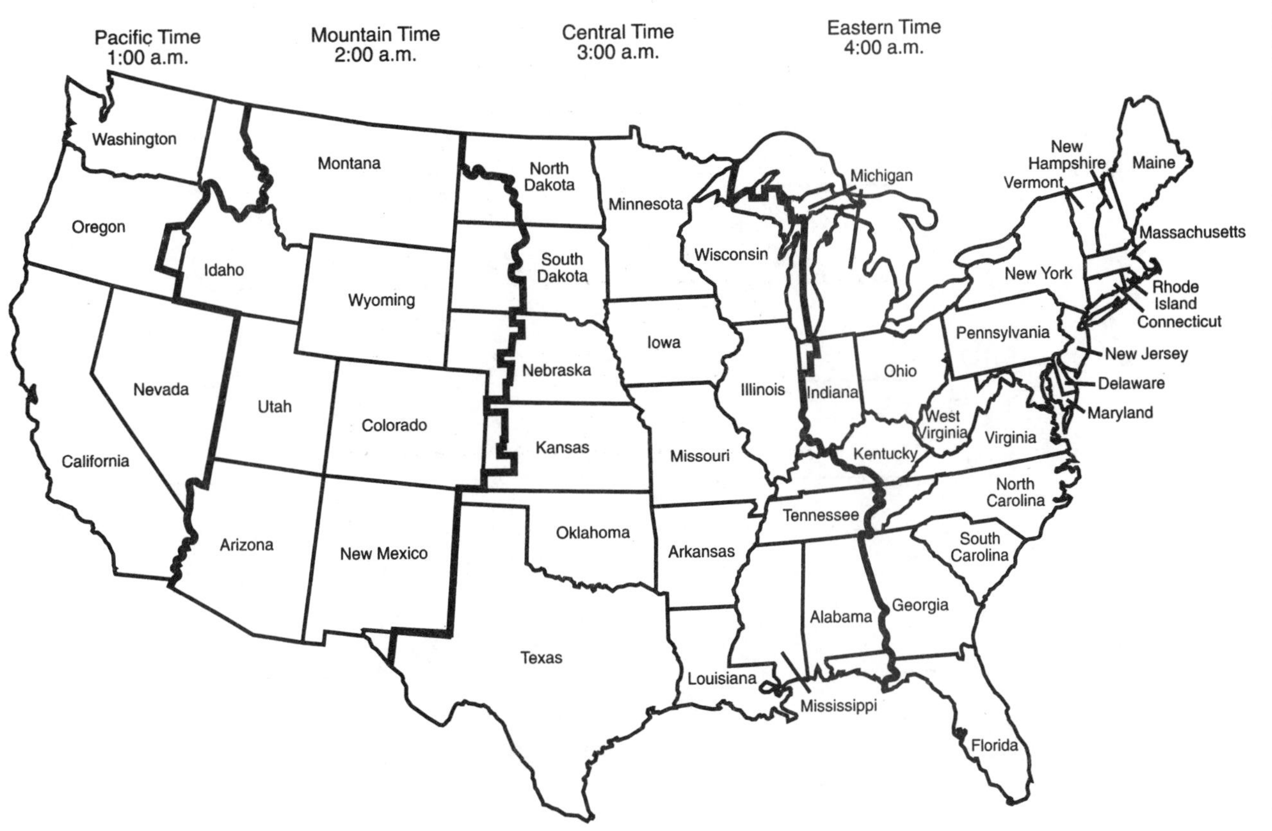

Name ____________________

Estimation

Estimate these sums and differences to the nearest hundred.

1. 459 + 392 ______
2. 328 + 987 ______
3. 109 + 450 ______
4. 943 + 661 ______
5. 780 + 453 ______
6. 853 + 349 ______
7. 953 + 1099 ______
8. 1052 + 342 ______
9. 1228 + 888 ______
10. 995 + 995 ______
11. 1499 + 549 ______
12. 4380 + 3291 ______
13. 2679 + 187 ______
14. 1982 + 76 ______
15. 1660 + 149 ______
16. 629 – 443 ______
17. 992 – 345 ______
18. 298 – 98 ______
19. 339 – 187 ______
20. 743 – 157 ______
21. 851 – 349 ______
22. 4682 – 597 ______
23. 7562 – 3415 ______
24. 1389 – 76 ______
25. 1982 – 1044 ______
26. 1995 – 1837 ______
27. 11,432 – 725 ______
28. 465 – 372 ______
29. 781 – 238 ______
30. 1068 – 1051 ______

Name________________________

SHARE

SHARE is a food and community program active in several states. Participants pay a fee and do community service in a wide variety of ways. Then, at the end of the month, the participants receive a box of groceries worth over twice what they paid. The difference between the money paid by the participants and the value of the food boxes is considered money saved by the participants. It is designed to make both the participants and communities winners.

Colorado is one of the states that has a SHARE program. Below is one of their monthly reports.

Number of SHARES: 24,038 (food boxes)
Dollars Saved: $432,684
Pounds of Food: 721,140
Retail Value: $745,178
Volunteer Hours: 72,114
Number of Host Sites: 295

1. How many pounds of food were in each food box? ________________
2. What was the retail value of each food box? ________________
3. How much money did each participant save? ________________
4. How much money did each participant pay for each food box? ________________
5. How many hours did each volunteer work this month? ________________
6. What is the average number of participants per host site? ________________

Name________________________

Three Shapes

Cut out the shapes on this page and put all of them together to make a rectangle. Rearrange the three pieces again to make a triangle. Rearrange the pieces one last time to make a parallelogram that is not a rectangle. Be prepared to show your teacher how you arranged the pieces to make each shape. You might want to draw diagrams to help you remember.

Name ____________________

Give a Call

Place an X on the map below to show where you live. Then use the map to help you answer the questions below.

There is a catalog from a Minnesota company from which you wish to order. They are only open from 8 a.m. to 5 p.m. Central Standard Time. Between what hours in your time zone can you reach them? ______ a.m. to ______ p.m.

A Seattle store's phone order department is open from Monday-Friday 6 a.m.-8 p.m. and Saturday 8 a.m.-4:30 p.m. Pacific Standard Time. To know when you can call them, change the hours to fit your time zone.

Mon.-Fri. ______ a.m. to ______ p.m.   Sat. ______ a.m. to ______ p.m.

A company giving national student exams is located in Princeton, NJ, with office hours from 9 a.m. to 4:30 p.m. Eastern Standard Time. Since your older sister needs to call them, change their hours to fit your time zone. ______ a.m. to ______ p.m.

You are going to call your friends who recently moved to Kalispell, MT. Your friend will be waiting for a phone call from 6 p.m. to 9:30 p.m. Mountain Standard Time. Between what hours in your time zone can you call? ______ a.m. to ______ p.m.

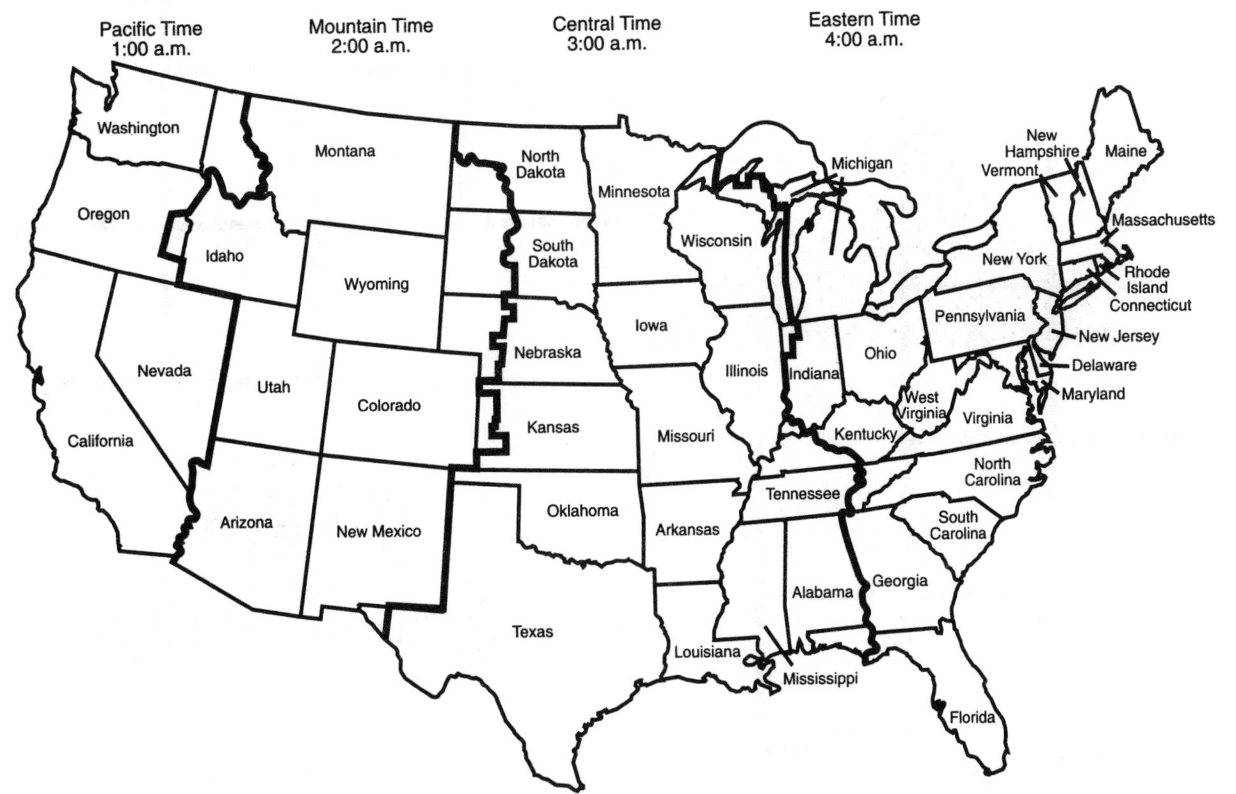

Name ________________________________

Math Box

Write the letters **M**, **T**, and **H** on figures 2 and 3 so that when the figure is folded into a box, it will spell MATH around the sides of the box. Figure 1 shows the correct placement of the letters. When you have placed the letters, cut out the shapes to see if you were right. If your were right, how did you decide on the letter placement? If you had trouble, what was the biggest problem?

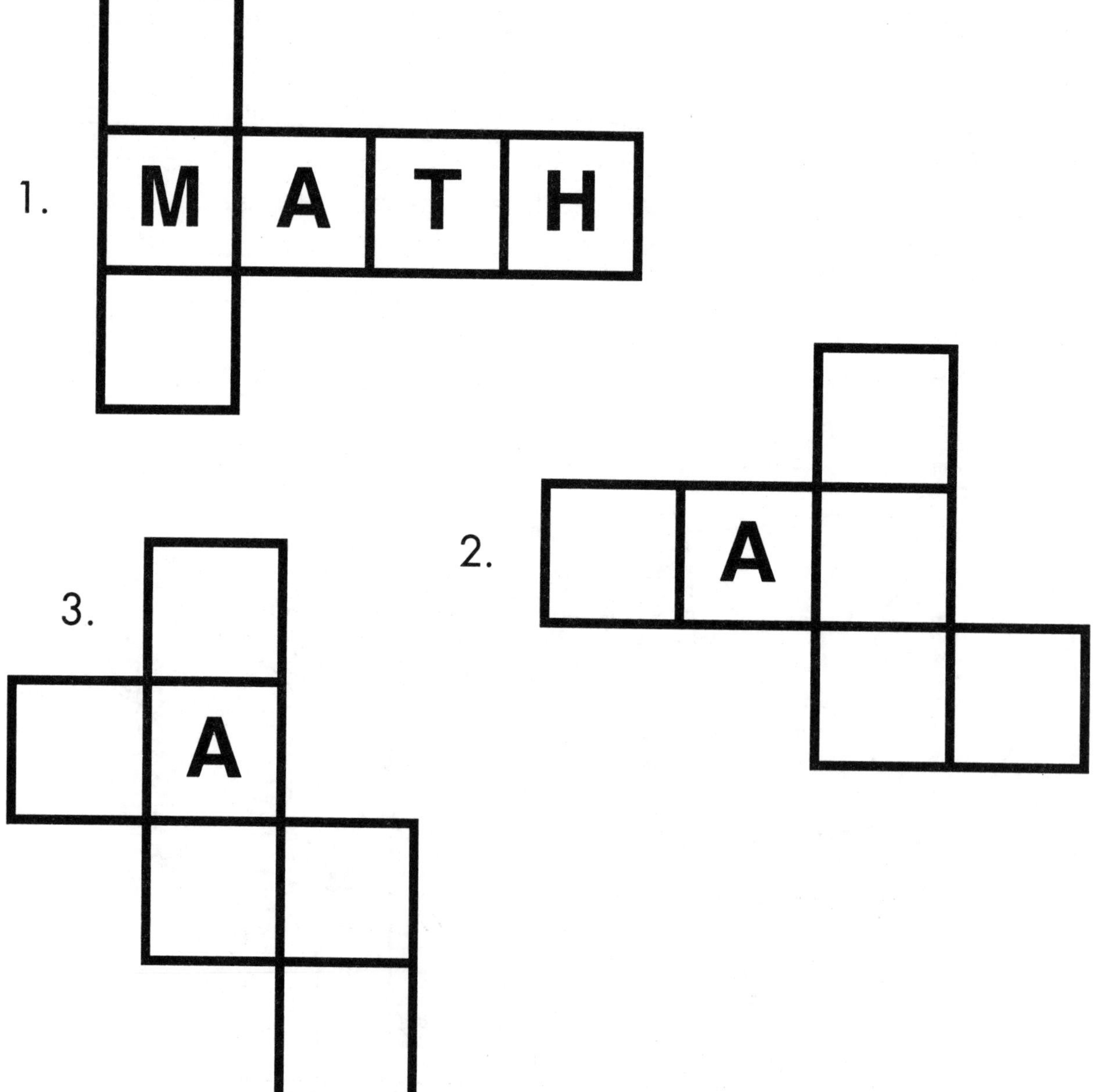

Name ______________________

Get Ready, Get Set...

Read each problem. Color in the answer on the hundred's chart. When you're finished, you'll know what to do after you "get set!"

1. Both numbers with a 2 and a 6
2. 245 ÷ 5
3. 4 x 14
4. Number of sides in 7 triangles
5. (4 x 2) x 8
6. 69 ÷ 3
7. 75 − 46
8. 19 + 3
9. 6 x 4
10. (6 x 9) + 5
11. (15 + 8) x 2
12. 14 + 47
13. 3 x 13
14. Both numbers with a 3 and a 6
15. (3 x 4 x 5) + 6
16. 17 x 3
17. 345 ÷ 5
18. 536 ÷ 8
19. 9 x 6
20. 117 − 76
21. 4 x 7
22. 55 − 11
23. (9 x 6) − 27
24. 89 − 58
25. 4 x 17
26. (6 x 7) + 1

1	2	3	4	5	6	7	8	9	10
11	12	13	14	15	16	17	18	19	20
21	22	23	24	25	26	27	28	29	30
31	32	33	34	35	36	37	38	39	40
41	42	43	44	45	46	47	48	49	50
51	52	53	54	55	56	57	58	59	60
61	62	63	64	65	66	67	68	69	70
71	72	73	74	75	76	77	78	79	80
81	82	83	84	85	86	87	88	89	90
91	92	93	94	95	96	97	98	99	100

Name ______________________________

Snow Survey

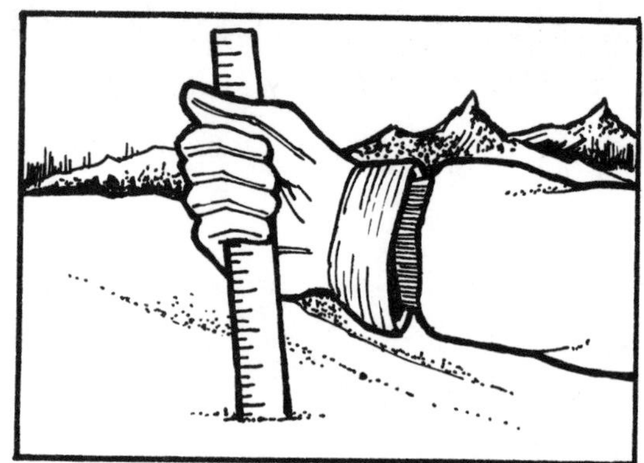

Some people think snow is important only during winter. However, snow is also very important to many people in the summer. The water that comes from the melting snow is critical for ranchers and farmers downstream as the water is stored and used through the summer months. So that everyone concerned may be aware of what the summer water situation will be, the winter snows are carefully monitored. Measurements are made of the snow depth and the water content of the snow.

Below are the records from three monitored sites in the Sangre de Cristo Mountains for the May 1st survey. Finish the records by figuring the percent of average and the percent of last year for both the snow depth and the water content. Use May 1995 for this year and May 1994 for last year. The numbers in the chart are in inches.

Huerfano	**May Average**	**May 1995**	**May 1994**	**% of Average**	**% of Last Year**
Snow Depth	31.5	41.5	35	________	________
Water Content	8.5	13.4	11.6	________	________
South Colony	**May Average**	**May 1995**	**May 1994**	**% of Average**	**% of Last Year**
Snow Depth	51	91.5	58	________	________
Water Content	18.9	37.2	19.3	________	________
Westcliffe	**May Average**	**May 1995**	**May 1994**	**% of Average**	**% of Last Year**
Snow Depth	7.3	26.5	7	________	________
Water Content	2.5	9.2	1.8	________	________

What is the water outlook for this year compared to last year? ______________________________

____

Name ____________________

Connect Odd

Circle the pairs of adjacent numbers in the rows below whose sum is odd when added together. For example, in row one, 5 and 6 should be circled as their sum is odd. But 6 and 8 should not be circled because their sum is even.

5 6 8 6 7 3 2 4 7 5 6 8 9 1 7 3 4 5 6 5

9 4 3 8 7 8 2 3 3 2 1 7 5 9 7 6 3 5 3 2

4 5 4 2 8 7 5 4 6 3 2 2 5 6 1 9 7 3 1 1

7 6 5 4 2 1 3 5 6 7 9 8 7 4 2 5 7 8 3 6

9 5 7 6 4 9 4 2 5 8 3 7 9 3 5 6 7 6 9 4

6 7 7 5 3 3 2 4 5 8 9 7 5 5 1 1 6 9 6 2

9 5 2 4 8 5 4 3 5 9 8 4 5 8 2 3 1 5 8 8

5 8 4 2 6 7 9 2 5 3 1 6 1 8 5 6 4 2 3 5

4 3 5 9 8 4 5 8 2 3 5 8 8 5 1 5 4 7 7 6

6 6 7 3 5 8 5 5 3 4 9 9 9 4 7 6 6 7 2 5

6 2 7 9 6 1 2 3 4 5 6 7 8 9 7 6 4 4 3 2

Is there a pattern? ____________________

____

Name ______________________________

Doing Darts

List all the possible scores you could get with four darts using the target below.

Possible Scores:

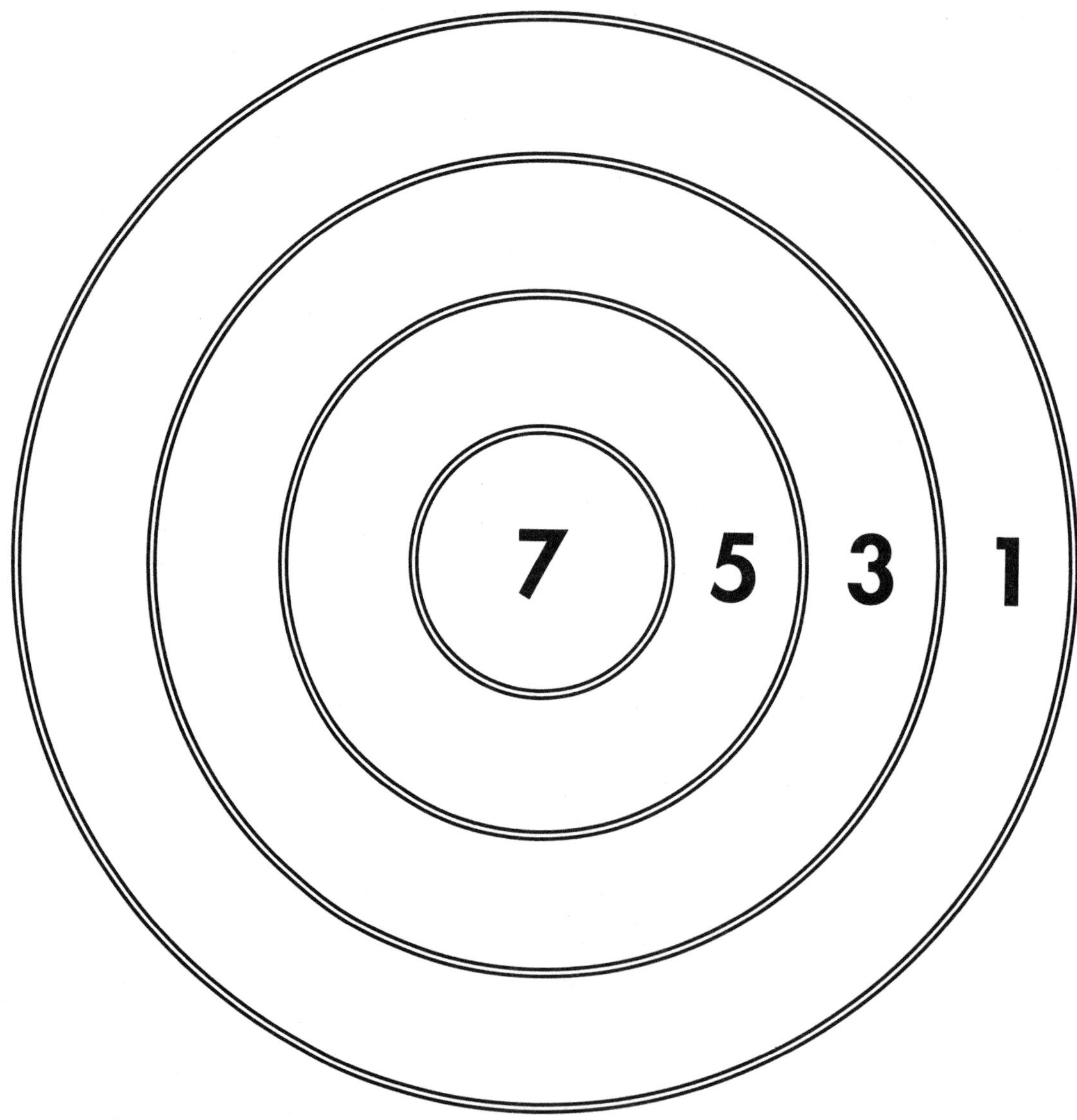

Name ____________________

A Pyramid

Cut out the two shapes below. Fold each shape on the dotted lines. Tape the edges of each shape together so you have two three-dimensional shapes, each with five faces. Here is your challenge: Fit the two shapes together so that you now have a pyramid.

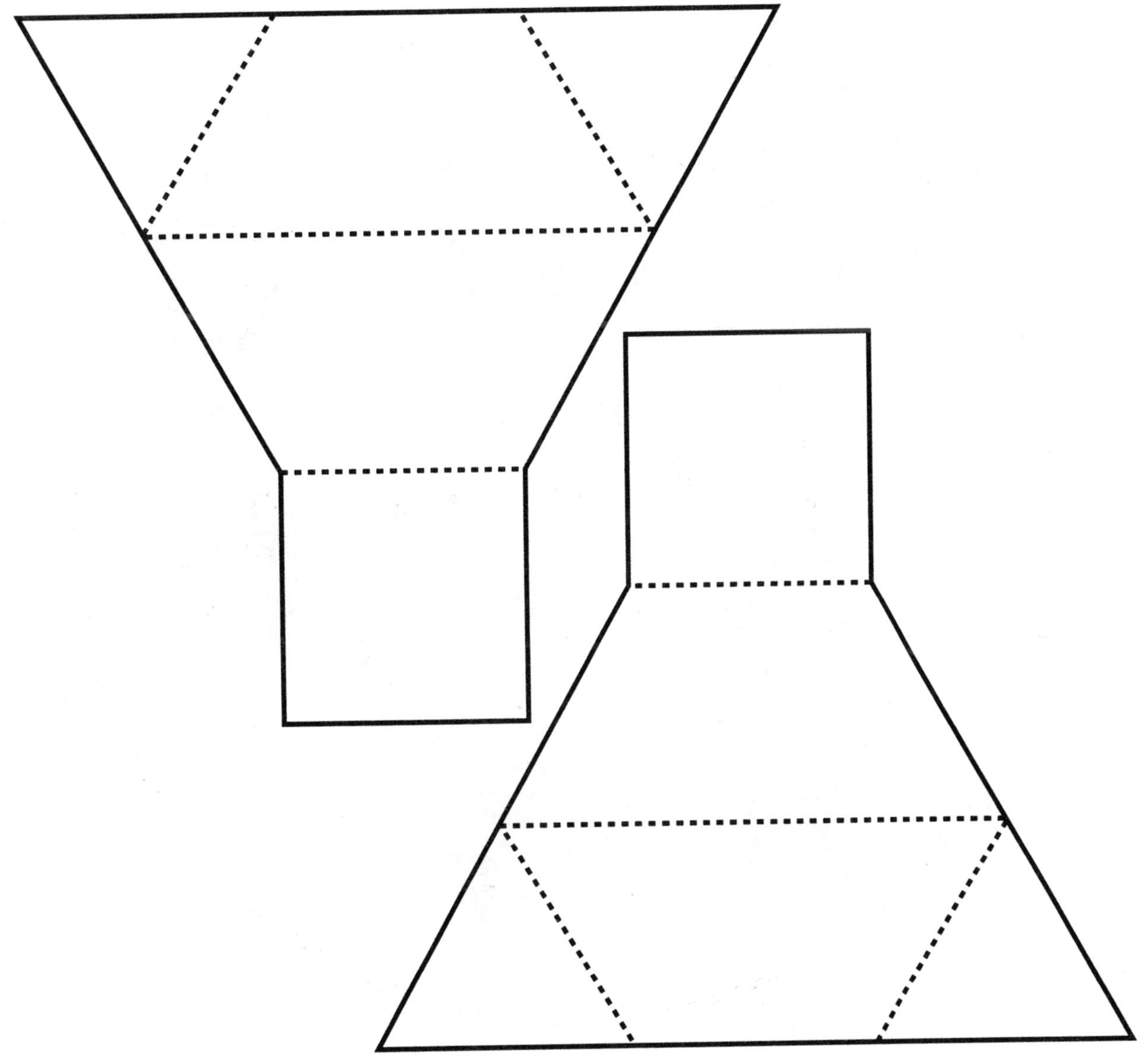

Name ____________________

Fraction Figuring

To solve this puzzle, choose a fraction to put in the empty squares. The three rows across and the three columns down must be correct number sentences. You may use any fraction more than once. The calculations must be performed one at a time and in the order given.

12	x		x		= 2
x		x		x	
	x	18	x		= 3
x		x		x	
	x		x	30	= 2
= 2		= 3		= 2	

Name ______________________

Four Shapes

Cut out the shapes on this page and put them together to make a square. You must use all three triangles. Then, rearrange the three pieces to make a rectangle that is not a square. Rearrange the pieces again to make a triangle. Rearrange the pieces one last time to make a parallelogram that is not a rectangle. Be prepared to show your teacher how you arranged the pieces to make each shape. You might want to draw diagrams to help you remember.

Name___________________________

A Six-Point Sum

Using each of the numbers from 1 to 12 exactly once, fill in the circles on this star so that the sum of the numbers in each row is 26.

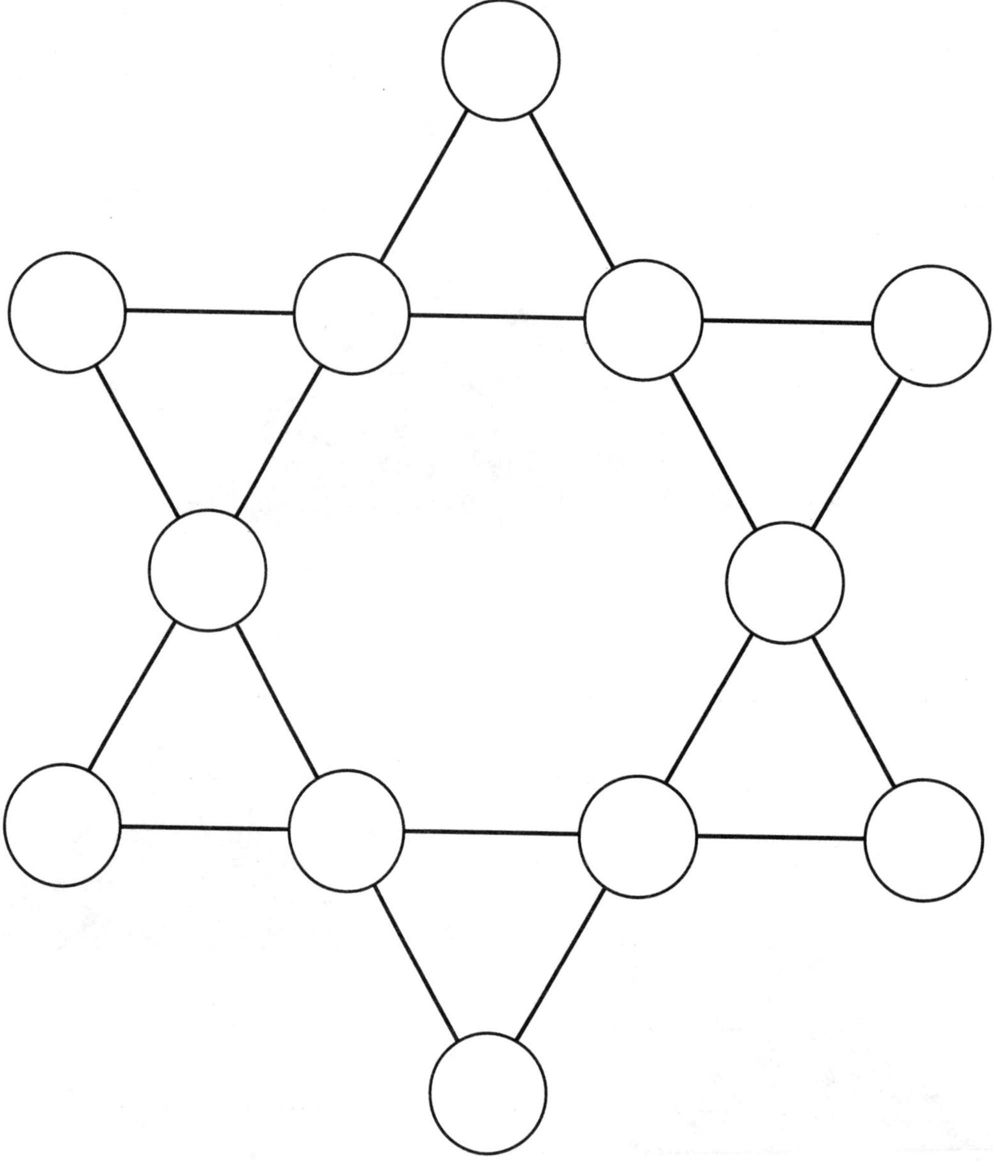

Name ____________________

Largest to Smallest

Put the numbers below in order with the largest on line 1 and the smallest on line 20.

$\frac{7}{6}$	$\frac{3}{10}$	$\frac{8}{3}$	0.06	$\frac{18}{10}$
$\frac{9}{7}$	$\frac{16}{15}$	$\frac{4}{5}$	$\frac{3}{6}$	$\frac{95}{1000}$
$\frac{95}{60}$	$\frac{9}{8}$	$3\frac{4}{5}$	$3\frac{5}{6}$	$\frac{52}{13}$
$\frac{39}{13}$	$\frac{7}{15}$	$\frac{8}{5}$	$\frac{4}{3}$	$\frac{11}{12}$

1. ____________________
2. ____________________
3. ____________________
4. ____________________
5. ____________________
6. ____________________
7. ____________________
8. ____________________
9. ____________________
10. ____________________
11. ____________________
12. ____________________
13. ____________________
14. ____________________
15. ____________________
16. ____________________
17. ____________________
18. ____________________
19. ____________________
20. ____________________

Name ____________________

Worth Its Weight

There is an old saying about something or someone being so valuable that it is worth its weight in gold. That means very valuable, but exactly how valuable is it?

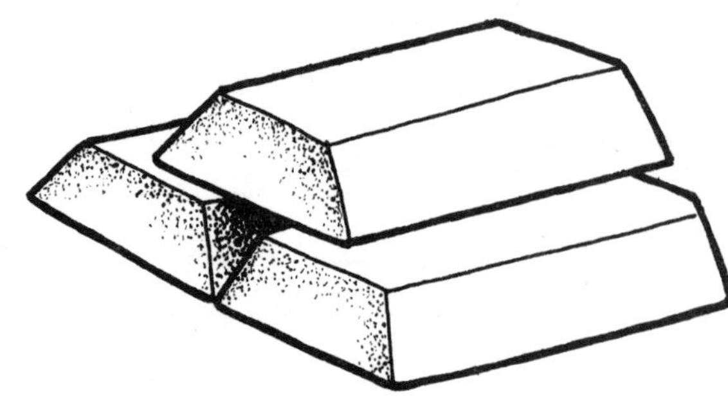

Precious metals are measured in troy ounces which are not the same as avoirdupois ounces that we commonly use in our everyday life. The weight of a troy ounce of gold is equal to 1.097 avoirdupois ounces. One avoirdupois once is equal to 0.911 troy ounce. While there are 16 avoirdupois ounces in an avoirdupois pound, there are only 12 troy ounces in a troy pound.

1. How much would a 125-pound person be worth in gold if gold is currently selling at $388.40 per troy ounce? ____________

While gold is a very valuable metal, it is not the most valuable. One metal selling for more than gold is platinum. On the same day that gold sells for $388.40 per troy ounce, platinum sells for $52.70 more per troy ounce!

2. What does a troy ounce of platinum cost? ____________
3. What would be the value of a 125-pound person worth his or her weight in platinum? ____________
4. By approximately what percentage does the value increase going from gold to platinum? ____________

Use other weights (sugar, canned goods, your little brother, etc.) to find the value in gold and/or platinum. Be ready to share some of your findings.

Name_______________

Who Owns What?

The U.S. Census reports that there were 91,947,000 households in the United States in 1991. Of these households, they report that:

75% owned a clothes washer
45% owned a dishwasher
79% owned a microwave oven
99% owned a television set
53% owned a clothes dryer

How many households do NOT own the items listed below? (Round your answer to the nearest thousand.)

clothes washer _______________

dishwasher _______________

microwave oven _______________

television set _______________

clothes dryer _______________

Name ______________________

Prime Numbers

More than 2000 years ago, a mathematician named Eratosthenes came up with a way to find all the prime numbers less than 100. Prime numbers are numbers whose only factors are 1 and the number itself. One is not prime or composite. It is unique and not included on this chart.

1. Circle 2. Cross out all multiples of 2.
2. Circle 3. Cross out all multiples of 3.
3. Circle the next number that is not crossed out—5. Cross out all multiples of 5.
4. Circle the next number that is not crossed out—7. Cross out all multiples of 7.
5. Circle the remaining numbers that are not crossed out. These are the prime numbers less than 100.
6. How many prime numbers are there? ______________________

	2	3	4	5	6	7	8	9	10
11	12	13	14	15	16	17	18	19	20
21	22	23	24	25	26	27	28	29	30
31	32	33	34	35	36	37	38	39	40
41	42	43	44	45	46	47	48	49	50
51	52	53	54	55	56	57	58	59	60
61	62	63	64	65	66	67	68	69	70
71	72	73	74	75	76	77	78	79	80
81	82	83	84	85	86	87	88	89	90
91	92	93	94	95	96	97	98	99	100

Name ______________________________

Sentence Stuff

Use the symbols below to fill in the blanks to make these number sentences true. The operations in the number sentences are to be done one at a time and in the order you put them in the sentences. These symbols may be used in any order and in any combination you wish.

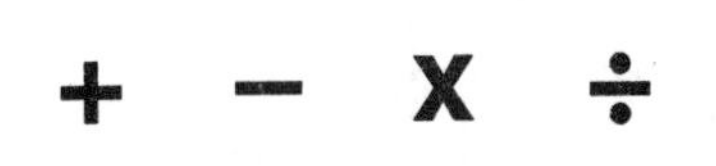

1. 1 ____ 2 ____ 3 ____ 4 = 2

2. 1 ____ 2 ____ 3 ____ 4 = 36

3. 2 ____ 3 ____ 4 ____ 5 = 4

4. 2 ____ 3 ____ 4 ____ 5 = 10

5. 3 ____ 4 ____ 5 ____ 6 = 10

6. 3 ____ 4 ____ 5 ____ 6 = 42

7. 4 ____ 5 ____ 6 ____ 7 = 21

8. 4 ____ 5 ____ 6 ____ 7 = 2

9. 5 ____ 6 ____ 7 ____ 8 = 0.5

10. 5 ____ 6 ____ 7 ____ 8 = 29

Name____________________________

The Cereal Box

The plot isn't very interesting, but the cereal box is still widely used for reading. Why? We're usually a captive audience as the box sits there in front of us as we eat breakfast. Sometimes there are puzzles and coupons put there by manufacturers. Nutritional information is usually on the side of the box.

1. As I read my cereal box, I find that it tells me that one serving is one cup or 30 grams. I turn to the front of the box and find the net weight listed at 283 grams. How many servings of cereal should I get from this box? __________

2. The nutritional information says that there are 110 calories per serving. How many calories are in this box? __________

3. As I read more, I find that my cup of cereal will give me 25% of the Vitamin A I need each day. How much cereal would I have to eat to get all of the Vitamin A I need each day? __________

4. Each serving of my cereal also gives me 4% of my daily need of calcium. How many servings of cereal should I eat to fill my total daily need of calcium?

   ____

5. Finally, I measured the box itself. It is 10 ¾ inches tall, 7 ½ inches wide, and 2 ¼ inches deep. What is the volume of this box in cubic inches? __________

Name ____________________

Complete the Number Sentence

Find at least three ways to get from the first number to the second number. The operations should be done consecutively and one at a time unless you note otherwise.

Example: 19 to 119
$19 \times 6 + 5 = 119$
$19 + 1 \times 6 - 1 = 119$
$19 \div 2 \times 13 - 4.5 = 119$

15 to 75 ____________________

____

____

12 to 136 ____________________

____

____

20 to 285 ____________________

____

____

16 to 76 ____________________

____

____

25 to 436 ____________________

____

____

Name ____________________

Who Made More?

Max kept records about where he spent his money. At the end of the year, he announced that he had spent ½ of his income on food and rent, ⅓ of his income on clothing, 1⁄12 on entertainment, and had saved $1400.

Mike said he had spent ½ of his income on food and rent, ¼ of his income on clothing, 1⁄12 on entertainment, and had saved $1400.

1. Who had the highest yearly salary? ____________________
2. How much more did he make? ____________________
3. How much did the other person make during the year? ____________________

Use the space below to explain how you arrived at your answer.

Name ____________________

Rectangle Challenge

It has been said that there are about 200 ways to put the pieces below together to make a rectangle. It is quite a challenge to find one way! Cut out the pieces below and move them around to make your rectangle. If you find one way, try to find another. Compare your rectangles with your classmates.

Name ____________________

Four Shapes Again

Cut out the shapes on this page and put them together to make a rectangle that is not a square. You must use all three shapes. Then, rearrange the three pieces to make a triangle. Rearrange the pieces again to make a parallelogram that is not a rectangle. Rearrange the pieces one last time to make a trapezoid that is neither a rectangle nor a parallelogram. Be prepared to show your teacher how you arranged the pieces to make each shape. You might want to draw diagrams to help you remember.

Answer Key

1 to 100—p. 1

Using the combinations of 1+99=100, 2+98=100, etc. you will find that up to 49, there is a combination for each number that =100. 49 x 100 = 4900. You then have used all the numbers 1-49 and 51-99. Then simply add the 50 and the 100 to 4900 and the answer is <u>5050</u>.

To find the answer to the sum of 1 to 200, use the combinations 1+199=200, 2+198=200, etc. All the numbers from 1-99 and 101-199 are part of combinations that =200. 99 x 200 = 19,800 Then add the 100 and the 200 to get the sum of <u>20,100</u>.

Organize the Classes—p. 3

One possible solution is:

Gr. 1 room:—24 - 1st-graders

Gr. 1/2 room:—11 - 1st-graders, 13 - 2nd-graders

Gr. 2/3 room:—13 - 2nd-graders, 9 - 3rd-graders

Gr. 2/3 room:—13 - 2nd-graders, 9 - 3rd-graders

Gr. 3/4 room:—11 - 3rd-graders, 13 - 4th-graders

Gr. 4/5 room:—20 - 4th-graders, 7 - 5th-graders

Gr. 5 room: 29 - 5th-graders

Whirlybird—p. 4

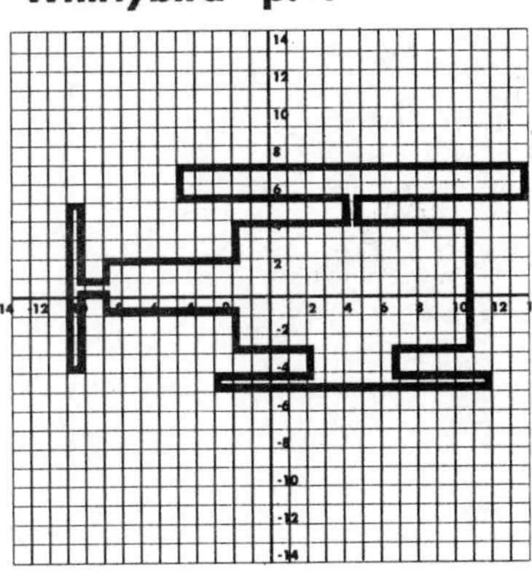

Checkerboard Squares—p. 5

Square Size	Number
1 x 1	64
2 x 2	49
3 x 3	36
4 x 4	25
5 x 5	16
6 x 6	9
7 x 7	4
8 x 8	1
Total	204

Make a Triangle—p. 6

A Record Flight—p. 7

1. 216 hours
2. 9 days
3. 5.5 miles per liter
4. 1203.84 gallons
5. 20.76 miles per gallon

Hey, Big Spender!—p. 8

<u>1 million dollars:</u>

16,666 minutes, 40 seconds

277 hours, 46 minutes, 40 seconds

11 days, 13 hours, 46 minutes, 40 seconds

<u>1 billion dollars:</u>

16,666,666 minutes, 40 seconds

277,777 hours, 46 minutes, 40 seconds

11,574 days, 1 hour, 46 minutes, 40 seconds

31 years, 259 days, 1 hour, 46 minutes, 40 seconds

(using 365 days in a year)

T-Time—p. 9

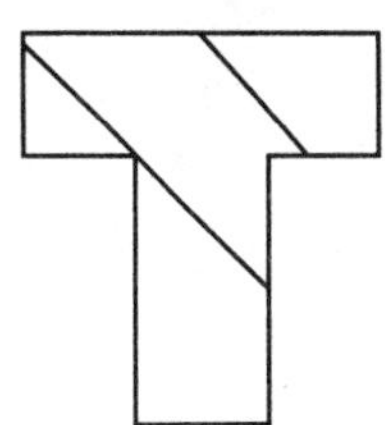

Find the Area—p. 11

A.1. 4 sq. units 2. 4 sq. units
3. 2 sq. units 4. 1 sq. unit
5. 2 sq. units 6. 1 sq. unit
7. 2 sq. units

B.1. 8 sq. units 2. 8 sq. units
3. 4 sq. units 4. 2 sq. units
5. 4 sq. units 6. 2 sq. units
7. 4 sq. units

Whole figure: 32 sq. units

Consecutive Numbers—p. 12

1. 47, 48, 49
2. 46, 48, 50
3. 33, 35, 37, 39

Magic Square1—p. 13

Magic Sum: 40

8	11	16	5
6	12	13	9
12	8	7	13
14	9	4	13

Have a Heart—p. 14

1. 35 (34.5)
2. 4
3. 10
4. 75 gallons per hour
5. 1,800 gallons per day
6. 12,600 gallons per week
7. Answers will vary.
8. approximately 5 weeks

Make a Parallelogram—p. 15

More Consecutive Numbers—p. 16

1. 28, 29, 30, 31, 32
2. 26, 28, 30, 32, 34
3. 37, 39, 41, 43

Up and Down—p. 17

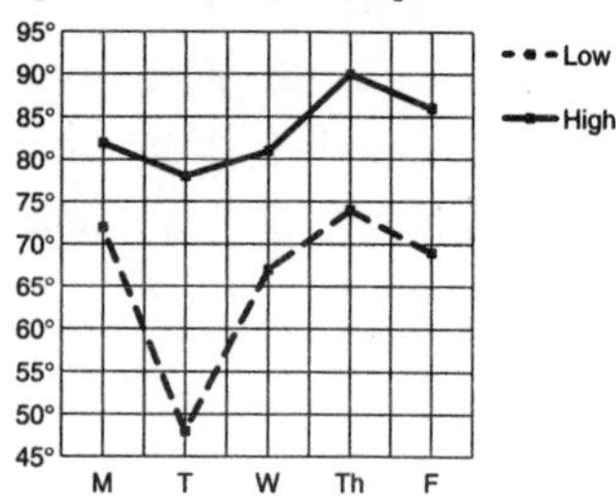

Average difference between highs and lows: 17.4°

Magic Square 2—p. 18

Magic Sum: 35

One solution is below. Students may have others.

8	11	6	10
7	6	9	13
11	7	13	4
9	11	7	8

Tile Time—p. 19

Wall 1 needs 44 tiles.
Wall 2 needs 242 tiles.
Wall 3 needs 132 tiles.
Wall 4 needs 88 tiles.
Total tiles needed: 506
Cost: $247.94

Brick Diamond—p. 20

1. $643,200
2. 32 square inches
3. 274,432 square inches
4. approximately 1905 sq. ft.
5. approximately 44 (43.7) feet on each side

A Friendly Puzzle—p. 21

1	2	3	4	5	6	7	8	9	10
11	12	13	14	15	16	17	18	19	20
21	22	23	24	25	26	27	28	29	30
31	32	33	34	35	36	37	38	39	40
41	42	43	44	45	46	47	48	49	50
51	52	53	54	55	56	57	58	59	60
61	62	63	64	65	66	67	68	69	70
71	72	73	74	75	76	77	78	79	80
81	82	83	84	85	86	87	88	89	90
91	92	93	94	95	96	97	98	99	100

Change a Square—p. 22

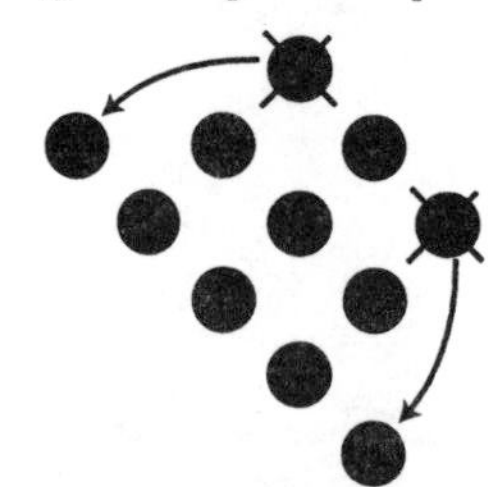

Make a Square—p. 24

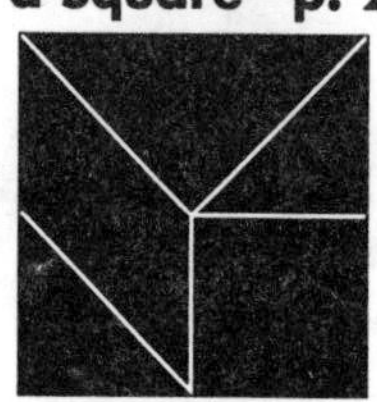

Figure the Area—p. 25

A = 81 square units
B = 25 square units
C = 36 square units
D = 49 square units
E = 1 square unit
F = 16 square units
G = 64 square units
H = 25 square units

Power Outage—p. 26

1. The electric clock starts from the time the electricity went out. The power was out for 43 minutes which is the difference between the wristwatch and the electric clock.
2. The digital clock starts at 12:00 so back up 6:20 from 4:58 (current accurate time) and you will know that the electricity came back on at 10:38.
3. Back up 43 minutes from 10:38 and the electricity went off at 9:55.

Start With a Penny—p. 27

After 30 days, Dad's plan would pay $300 (30 days x $10 each day). After 30 days, Sam's plan would pay $5,368,709.12 on the 30th day.

Mystery Numbers—p. 28

1. Keys on a Piano
2. Buttons on a Phone
3. Degrees Fahrenheit at which Water Freezes
4. Digits in a Zip Code
5. Sides on a Stop Sign
6. Innings in a Ball Game
7. Quarters in a Dollar
8. Feet in a Mile
9. Dollars for Passing Go in Monopoly
10. Yards on a Football Field
11. Feet Between Bases on a Baseball Field
12. Planets in the Solar System
13. Eggs in a Dozen
14. Degrees in a Circle
15. Holes in Golf

Tournament Planning—p. 29

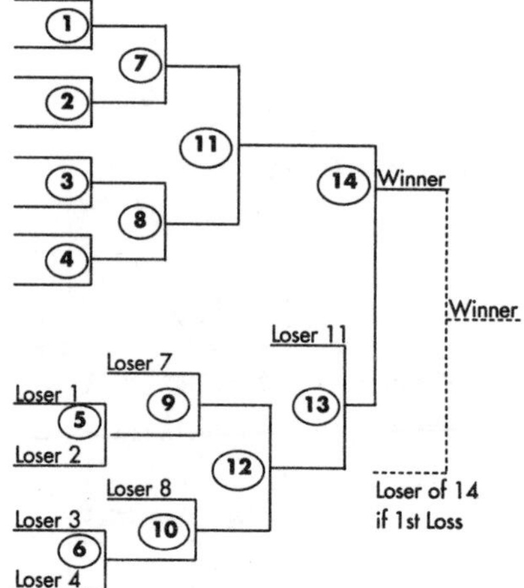

Give Me the Odds—p. 30

The sum of the first 25 odd counting numbers is 625. The sum of the first 5 odd numbers is 25. The sum of the next 5 odd numbers is 75. The sum of the next 5 odd numbers is 125. The pattern is adding 50 to the previous total to get the total for the next group of 5 odd numbers. 25 + 75 + 125 + 175 + 225 = 625. The sum of the first 25 even counting numbers is 650. The sum of the first 5 even counting numbers is 30. The sum of the next 5 even counting numbers is 80. Again the pattern of adding 50 to the previous sum. 30 + 80 + 130 + 180 + 230 = 650.

It is quite possible that the students may come up with other strategies.

Windchill Factor—p. 31

Air Temperature (°F)	Wind speed in miles per hour								
	0	5	10	15	20	25	30	35	40
	Apparent or "Feels Like" Temperature								
35	35	32	22	16	12	8	6	4	3
30	30	27	16	9	4	1	2	-4	-5
25	25	22	10	2	-3	-7	-10	-12	-13
20	20	16	3	-5	-10	-15	-18	-20	-21
15	15	11	-3	-11	-17	-22	-25	-27	-29
10	10	6	-9	-18	-24	-29	-33	-35	-37
5	5	0	-15	-25	-31	-36	-41	-43	-45
0	0	-5	-22	-31	-39	-44	-49	-52	-53
-5	-5	-10	-27	-38	-46	-51	-56	-58	-60
-10	-10	-15	-34	-45	-53	-59	-64	-67	-69
-15	-15	-21	-40	-51	-60	-66	-71	-74	-76
-20	-20	-26	-46	-58	-67	-74	-79	-82	-84
-25	-25	-31	-52	-65	-74	-81	-86	-89	-92

Highest Temperature: 40°

Lowest Wind Speed: 5 m.p.h.

Graph It Smaller—p. 32

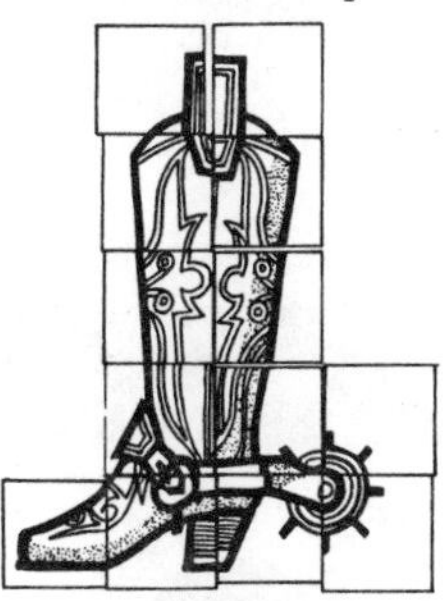

Combination Count—p. 33

There are 72 different 2-digit numbers possible. One possible strategy: List the possibilities for 1 with the other numbers, 2 with the other numbers, etc., and find a pattern.

Post Time—p. 34

1. 22 fence posts
2. $115.50

Make a Rectangle—p. 35

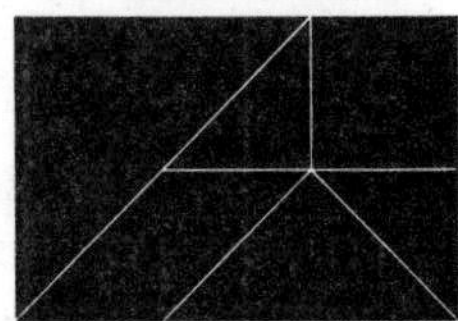

Shelly's French Fries—p. 36

1. 1600 potatoes
2. 800 orders
3. 1 ton or 2000 pounds
4. 52 tons or 104,000 pounds
5. 4000 orders
6. 208,000 orders
7. $320 8. $16,640
9. $18,200

How Many Miles?—p. 37

1. 28.6 2. 27.3
3. 29.7 4. 31.6
5. 30.1 6. 28.3
7. 23.4 8. 28.4

Don't Touch!—p. 38

Choose Your Pay—p. 39

Choice 1:

Year 1—25,000

Year 2—26,000

Year 3—27,000

Year 4—28,000

Year 5—29,000

Choice 2

Year 1—
12,500 + 12,750 = 25,250

Year 2—
13,000 + 13,250 = 26,250

Year 3—
13,500 + 13,750 = 27,250

Year 4—
14,000 + 14,250 = 28,250

Year 5—
14,500 + 14,750 = 29,250

Choice 2 will have paid $1,250 more after 5 years.

Geometry Vocabulary—p. 40

H	C	Q	O	P	T	N	E	U	R	G	N	O	C	C
W	E	I	U	V	N	O	G	A	T	C	O	R	U	C
L	D	X	R	A	A	B	D	K	Y	V	A	R	O	P
L	O	S	A	C	D	L	L	Z	G	L	V	N	E	A
A	D	Y	H	G	L	R	W	J	U	E	E	U	L	R
T	E	M	E	V	O	E	I	C	C	P	D	G	G	A
N	C	M	V	A	M	N	I	L	D	I	R	L	N	L
O	A	E	C	T	D	D	R	N	A	B	J	N	A	L
Z	G	T	Z	V	N	E	H	N	O	T	M	N	I	E
I	O	R	L	E	D	S	O	D	P	G	E	O	R	L
R	N	Y	P	N	Q	N	O	F	Y	R	A	R	T	H
O	R	R	I	U	A	N	T	B	F	D	I	C	A	P
H	E	L	A	G	P	Y	R	A	M	I	D	S	E	L
P	Y	R	O	P	E	N	T	A	G	O	N	G	M	D
C	E	N	N	O	I	T	A	L	L	E	S	S	E	T

No Word Problems—p 41

1. 8 Days – 24 Hours = 1 Week
2. 4 Pair = Eight
3. 104 Years – 4 Years = 1 Century
4. Seven – 7 = Zero
5. 2 Pints = 1 Quart
6. Square Root of 4 = Two
7. 1 + 3 Zeros = 1 Thousand
8. Pennies & Nickels & Dimes & Quarters & Half Dollars are all Coins.
9. Four x Two = Eight
10. 1 Decade + 1 Decade = 1 Score
11. 60 Seconds + 60 Seconds = 2 Minutes
12. 1 Hundred ÷ Five = Twenty
13. 3 Blind Mice + 3 Little Pigs = 6 Animals
14. Ten x Ten = 1 Hundred
15. One + Two + Three + Four = Ten

Palindromes—p. 42

Possible answers include:

3-step—786, 194, 86

4-step—571, 638, 699

5-step—176, 738, 297

6-step—988, 182, 97

7-step—782, 296, 190

Even Money—p.43

One solution:

25¢	10¢	5¢	1¢
1¢	5¢	10¢	25¢
10¢	25¢	1¢	5¢
5¢	1¢	25¢	10¢

The Recording Industry—p. 44

1975 sales: 437,200,000
Singles: 37.5%
Albums: 58.8%
Compact Discs: 0%
Cassettes: 3.7%

1980 sales: 597,300,000
Singles: 27.5%
Albums: 54%
Compact Discs: 0%
Cassettes: 18.5%

1985 sales: 649,400,000
Singles: 18.6%
Albums: 25.7%
Compact Discs: 3.5%
Cassettes: 52.2%

1990 sales: 768,000,000
Singles: 3.6%
Albums: 1.5%
Compact Discs: 37.3%
Cassettes: 57.6%

Receiving Change—p. 45

Coin combinations may vary.

1. Change: $.83—
   3 quarters, 1 nickel,
   3 pennies
2. Change: $2.62—
   2 $1 bills, 2 quarters,
   1 dime, 2 pennies
3. Change: $1.77—
   1 $1 bill, 3 quarters,
   2 pennies
4. Change: $3.61—
   3 $1 bills, 2 quarters,
   1 dime, 1 penny
5. Change: $.94—
   3 quarters, 1 dime,
   1 nickel, 4 pennies

Working Together—p. 46

Jerry painted $\frac{1}{6}$ of the house in one day. Jeff painted $\frac{1}{4}$ of the house in one day. Change these fractions to a common denominator. Jerry painted $\frac{2}{12}$ of the house in one day. Jeff painted $\frac{3}{12}$ of the house in one day. Together they painted $\frac{5}{12}$ of the house in one day, $\frac{10}{12}$ in two days, leaving $\frac{2}{12}$ or $\frac{1}{6}$ for the third day. Answer: 2 $\frac{1}{6}$ days

Heat Index—p. 47

Relative Humidity	Air Temperature 75°	80°	85°	90°	95°	100°	105°	110°	115°	120°
0%	69	73	78	83	87	91	95	99	103	107
10%	70	75	80	85	90	95	100	105	111	116
20%	72	77	82	87	93	99	105	112	120	130
30%	73	78	84	90	96	104	113	123	135	148
40%	74	79	86	93	101	110	123	137	151	
50%	75	81	88	96	107	120	135	150		
60%	76	82	90	100	114	132	149			
70%	77	85	93	106	124	144				
80%	78	86	97	113	136					
90%	79	88	102	122						
100%	80	91	108							

1. 85°
2. 0%
3. 80°
4. 0%

Square Where?—p. 48

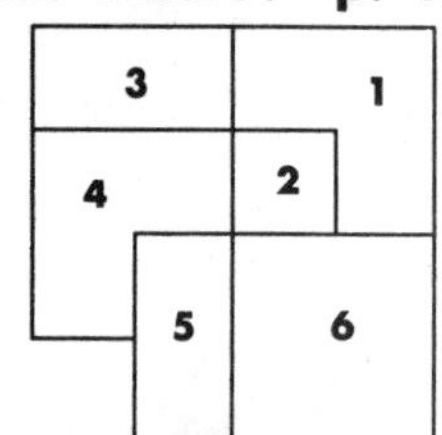

Make a Trapezoid—p. 49

Do I Use It?—p. 50

Daily use of the world of math for students would include a variety of things including, but not limited to, page numbers, locker numbers and combinations, time, lunches cooked at correct temperature, lunch money, scheduling, etc.

Television Ratings—p. 51

1. 15.1 million
2. 13.6 million
3. 13.3 million
4. 13.1 million
5. 12 million
6. 11.5 million
7. 11.4 million
9. 11.1 million
10. 11 million

ABC—Rating 12.4
Homes—11.8 million
CBS—Rating 11.6
Homes—11.1 million
NBC—Rating 13.9
Homes—13.3 million

Line Layout—p. 52

Buy a Pass—p. 53

1. $34
2. $1.70
3. $21.25
4. $1.06
5. $48
6. $1.60
7. $30
8. $1

Find Their Places—p. 54

One possible solution:

Rectangle/Triangle—p. 55

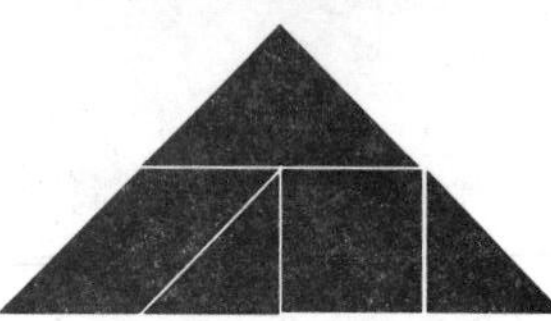

Tony's Commercials—p. 56

1. $4,869
2. $3,444
3. $19,344
4. 47 times
5. 30 times

Howard the Humongous—p. 57

At least 500 carrots should make it to market. Some students may be able to get more.

Multiply Odd—p. 58

To get an odd product, you must multiply two odd numbers. Two even numbers, and an odd number and an even number multiplied together give an odd product. There are 45 odd products.

Figure It Out—p. 59

One possible solution is:

5	x	3	-	6	= 9
+		+		-	
5	+	1	-	4	= 2
+		+		-	
2	x	3	+	1	= 7
= 5		= 7		= 1	

How Many Squares?—p. 60

9

Show One Half—p. 61

Possible answers:

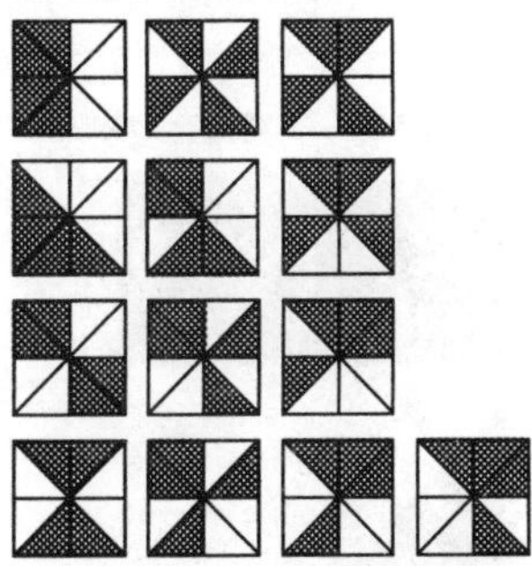

Another Figure It Out—p. 62

One possible solution is:

3	x	6	÷	9	= 2
-		+		-	
2	+	5	-	1	= 6
+		-		-	
6	+	4	-	5	= 5
= 7		= 7		= 3	

Paint Power—p. 63

1. 367.5 square feet
2. 1 gallon
3. ceiling: 2 quarts
   walls: 3 quarts
4. Approximately 23.5%
5. $12.99
6. $17.80

How Many Triangles—p.64

There are 47 triangles.

25: 1 x 1; 13: 2 x 2
6: 3 x 3; 2: 4 x 4; 1: 5 x 5

Flight Time—p. 65

Shortest time: Flight 1
4 hours 21 minutes

Longest time: Flight 4
5 hours 37 minutes

Estimation—p. 66

1. 900
2. 1300
3. 600
4. 1600
5. 1300
6. 1200
7. 2100
8. 1400
9. 2100
10. 2000
11. 2000
12. 7700
13. 2900
14. 2100
15. 1800
16. 200
17. 700
18. 200
19. 100
20. 500
21. 600
22. 4100
23. 4200
24. 1300
25. 1000
26. 200
27. 10,700
28. 100
29. 600
30. 0

SHARE—p. 67

1. 30 pounds
2. $31
3. $18
4. $13
5. 3 hours
6. 81-82 participants

Three Shapes—p. 68

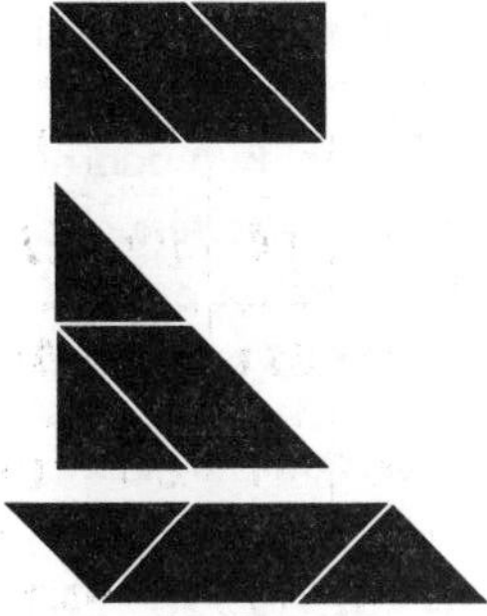

Math Box—p. 70

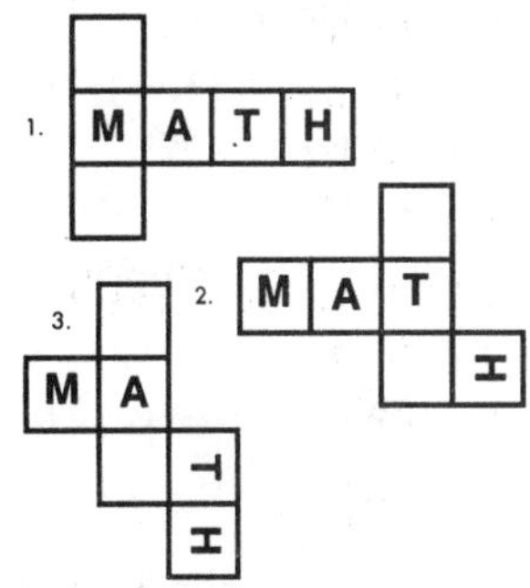

Get Ready, Get Set...—p. 71

1	2	3	4	5	6	7	8	9	10
11	12	13	14	15	16	17	18	19	20
21	22	23	24	25	26	27	28	29	30
31	32	33	34	35	36	37	38	39	40
41	42	43	44	45	46	47	48	49	50
51	52	53	54	55	56	57	58	59	60
61	62	63	64	65	66	67	68	69	70
71	72	73	74	75	76	77	78	79	80
81	82	83	84	85	86	87	88	89	90
91	92	93	94	95	96	97	98	99	100

Snow Survey—p. 72

<u>Huerfano</u>

Snow Depth:	132% of average 119% of last year
Water Content:	158% of average 116% of last year

<u>South Colony</u>

Snow Depth:	179% of average 158% of last year
Water Content:	197% of average 193% of last year

<u>Westcliffe</u>

Snow Depth:	363% of average 379% of last year
Water Content:	368% of average 511% of last year

Connect Odd—p. 73

To get an odd sum, you must add an odd number and an even number. Two odd numbers or two even numbers added together have an even sum. There are 116 odd sums.

Doing Darts—p. 74

There are 15 possible scores: 28, 26, 24, 22, 20, 19, 18, 17, 16, 14, 12, 10, 8, 6, 4.

A Pyramid—p. 75

Place the two shapes together so that the squares are touching each other. Then rotate one of the shapes, and a pyramid will appear.

Fraction Figuring—p. 76

One possible solution is:

12	x	$\frac{1}{2}$	x	$\frac{1}{3}$	= 2
x		x		x	
$\frac{5}{6}$	x	18	x	$\frac{1}{5}$	= 3
x		x		x	
$\frac{1}{5}$	x	$\frac{1}{3}$	x	30	= 2
= 2		= 3		= 2	

Four Shapes—p. 77

A Six-Point Sum—p. 78

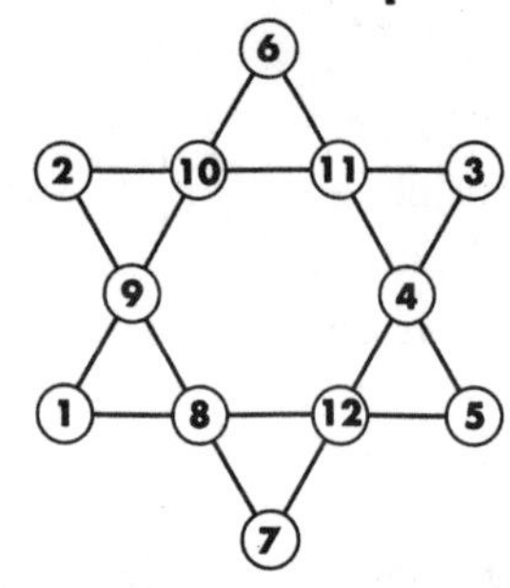

Largest to Smallest—p. 79

1. 52/13 (4)
2. 3 5/6 ($3.8\overline{3}$)
3. 3 4/5 (3.8)
4. 39/13 (3)
5. 8/3 ($2.\overline{6}$)
6. 18/10 (1.8)
7. 8/5 (1.6)
8. 95/60 ($1.58\overline{3}$)
9. 4/3 ($1.\overline{3}$)
10. 9/7 (1.285...)
11. 7/6 ($1.1\overline{6}$)
12. 9/8 (1.125)
13. 16/15 ($1.0\overline{6}$)
14. 11/12 ($0.91\overline{6}$)
15. 4/5 (0.8)
16. 3/6 (0.5)
17. 7/15 ($0.4\overline{6}$)
18. 3/10 (0.3)
19. 95/1000 (0.095)
20. 0.06

Worth Its Weight—p. 80

1. $707,664.80
2. $441.10 per troy ounce
3. $803,684.20
4. approximately 14%

Who Owns What?—p. 81

Households NOT owning:
clothes washer—22,987,000
dishwasher—50,571,000
microwave oven—19,309,000
television set—919,000
clothes dryer—43,215,000

Prime Numbers—p. 82

The 25 prime numbers are: 2, 3, 5, 7, 11, 13, 17, 19, 23, 29, 31, 37, 41, 43, 47, 53, 59, 61, 67, 71, 73, 79, 83, 89, 97.

Sentence Stuff—p. 83

1. 1 + 2 + 3 − 4 = 2
2. 1 + 2 x 3 x 4 = 36
3. 2 + 3 x 4 ÷ 5 = 4
4. 2 x 3 − 4 x 5 = 10
5. 3 x 4 x 5 ÷ 6 = 10
6. 3 x 4 - 5 x 6 = 42
7. 4 + 5 − 6 x 7 = 21
8. 4 x 5 − 6 ÷ 7 = 2
9. 5 + 6 − 7 ÷ 8 = 0.5
10. 5 x 6 + 7 − 8 = 29

The Cereal Box—p. 84

1. Approximately 9 ½ servings
2. Approximately 1045 calories
3. 4 cups
4. 25 cups
5. 181 ½ cubic inches

Who Made More?—p. 86

1. Max who made $16,800
2. $8,400
3. Mike made $8,400.

Rectangle Challenge—p. 87

One possible solution:

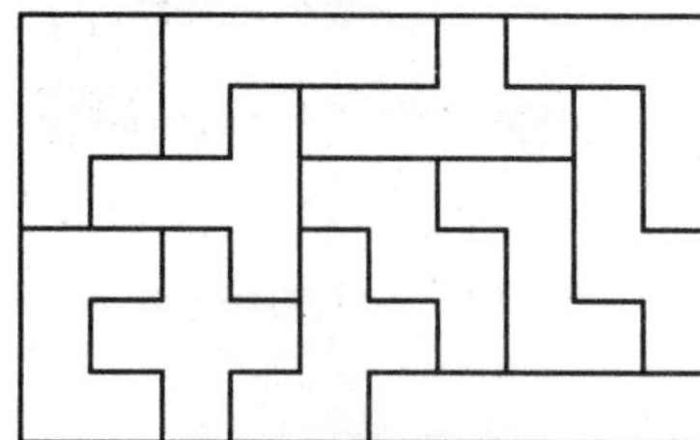

Four Shapes Again—p. 88